THE
SUCCESS
START

7 Practices to Make a Life of Significance

JUAN CARLOS ARZOLA

"The Success Start *is filled with an immense supply of encouragement, powerful quotes and stimulating bible verses that will support anyone who is searching to live a better life.*"

> – Linda McLean, CEO & Founder, McLean International and
> #1 International Best Selling Author

"*Juan Carlos provides clear, succinct and very useful habits that anyone can implement.* The Success Start *aims to make the reader realize that success begins in your own mind. This book will guide you on how to be more conscious of what you think, and how to transform negative thoughts into positive ones, thus taking you one step closer to success! A must read for every human being out there!.*"

> – Judy O'Beirn, Creator and Co-Author of the International Bestselling
> Series, *Unwavering Strength*

Juan Carlos Arzola speaks from his heart in his uplifting book The Success Start, *sharing both spiritual and personal encouragement to help you reach your very best.*

> – Anne Karklins, Designer, Hasmark Publishing

"The Success Start *is a powerful book for anyone who wants to be successful. It focuses on the most important/vital element in a human body: the mind. This book helped me to be more aware of what thoughts I have about my life and myself, and inspired me to continue to pursue my dreams and never stop believing that whatever I want to do, I can do. Everyone should read this book as it applies to all of us.*"

> – Jenn Gibson, Co-Author of *Unwavering Strength Series*

"*Juan Carlos is one of a kind. When you meet him you will never forget his smile, his heart for others and his genuineness to become the greatest version of himself.* The Success Start *isn't an option if you want to lead a life worth living. Statistics say that 98% of the world is drifting through life. What if you could escalate your promotion, raise, increase or explosion?* The Success Start *is your "what if." Get ready, buckle up and make sure to ask yourself... "do I really want to open this door?" Your life begins now.*"

> – Daniel J Budzinski, Director, Compassionate Touch International,
> www.ctinternational.org

Published by
Hasmark Publishing
judy@hasmarkpublishing.com

Editor: Nita Robinson
nita@helpinghand.com

Cover Design: Patti Knoles
patti@virtualgraphicartsdepartment.com

Layout: Anne Karklins
annekarklins@gmail.com

ISBN-13: 978-1-988071-33-6
ISBN-10: 198807133X

General & Legal Disclaimer

The information contained in or made available by the Promoter, Juan Carlos Arzola, or any third-party through this Book/Ebook, seminar or their websites or services cannot replace or substitute for the services of trained professionals in any medical or health field, including, but not limited to medical doctor, licensed psychologist, psychotherapist, psychiatrist or neuroscientist. Promoter does not offer any professional personal, medical or health advice and none of the information contained herein or in his programs should be confused as such advice. Neither Promoter, Juan Carlos Arzola nor their assigns, sponsors, speakers, partners, contractors, employees or any of their affiliates will be liable for any direct, indirect, consequential, special, exemplary or other damages to you or your business, including economic loss, that may result from information herein or participation in any Seminar or from the use of, or the inability to use, the materials, information, or strategies communicated through the this Book/Ebook, seminar, websites or any products or services provided pursuant to the Seminar, even if advised of the possibility of such damages. Under no circumstances, including but not limited to negligence, will Promoter or Juan Carlos Arzola be liable for any special or consequential damages that result from your use of the information or participation in the Seminar. To be clear: You, alone are responsible and accountable for your decisions, actions and results in life, and by your participation in our Seminar, you agree not to attempt to hold us, the Promoter or Juan Carlos Arzola, liable for any decisions, actions or results that you make or experience in business or in life due to your use of this Book/Ebook or participation in this Seminar at any time, under any circumstance.

YOU should seek specific professional counsel (mental, medical, physical or spiritual) that considers their specific facts and circumstances any advice or discussions provided during the seminar and or on the website or other communications are SOLELY for illustrative purposes and do not necessarily consider all elements of an individual's situation especially because of the limited information available to Juan Carlos Arzola during the program. Additionally, there are no guarantees of results or other assurances of any of the advice given by Juan Carlos Arzola or any of his staff or agents. YOU understand that it is their sole responsibility to perform the appropriate due diligence and independent investigation of any and all decisions to be made with respect to your health including your spiritual, mental, emotional and physical body. We've taken every effort to ensure we accurately represent our information and its potential to help you grow, change , improve or transform yourself. However, there is no guarantee that you will grow, change, improve or transform using the techniques displayed here, and we do not purport this as a "get quick results scheme." Nothing here is a promise or guarantee of results or earnings. Your level of success in attaining similar results is dependent upon a number of factors including your skill, knowledge, ability, dedication, discipline, motivation, inspiration, business savvy, and financial situation. Because these factors differ according to individuals, we cannot guarantee your success, income level, or ability to grow, change, improve or transform yourself or earn revenue.

Dedication

To God –
Thank you for opening my heart, for expanding my mind and for awakening my soul. Thank you for all that I have received and for the miracles unfolding. Thank you for the chance to make a difference.

To my children Juan Carlitos and Danielito –
Thank you for coming to this world. Thank you for letting me be your father and your friend. This is your book. This is your legacy. You are my legacy. May you always differentiate, be better and make a difference in this world. Always BE your best and DO your best for others, HAVE a life of success and significance and remember to GIVE back to the world.

To my mom Leyla –
Thank you for bringing me into this world, trusting me, and making me the person that I am today.

To my dad Carlos –
Thank you for giving me the greatest gift anyone could get; you believe in me.

To my sister Katty –
Thank you for being there in my triumphs and struggles, in my joy and pain.

To my brother Jose –
Thank you for your unconditional love, humbleness, your high moral values and being there when I needed you the most.

Acknowledgements

In preparing this book, I have received assistance directly and indirectly from many people including some of my coaches, trainers and mentors John Maxwell, Bob Proctor, Brendon Burchard, Tony Robbins and Brian Tracy.

The first draft was constructively criticized by Carlos H. Arzola. Nor would the work have been possible without the cooperation, help and assistance of the great many experts in their fields including Linda McLean, Peggy McColl, Judy O'Beirn, Nita Robinson, Patti Knoles and Anne Karklins.

I would like to thank all people who helped out with this book without them even knowing in some way or another over ideas, moral support, motivation and great inspiration. Full acknowledgment of the debt which I owe to these great people is not possible. Lots of love, respect and gratitude to you all.

Finally, I want to thank those of you who are courageous enough to believe in themselves. You are the real reason I have written this book. Keep pushing, keep learning, keep growing and may God bless you.

Juan Carlos Arzola
Weston, Florida
June 2016

with John C. Maxwell   *with Bob Proctor*   *with Curtis Sliwa*   *with Dean Graziosi*

Foreword

Do you feel like you are successful in all areas of your life? Do you ask yourself, *'what is my purpose? Who do I really want to be? What do I really want in my life?'* Are you happy with your life and feel like you are living the life of your dreams? Or do you find yourself wanting to make changes but have no idea how to do it? What if I told you that this book can remove whatever obstacles your facing and can create a huge shift in your life? The Universe is full of choices that help you reach your potential and within you lies the power to transform your life and create anything you desire.

I have been in the personal development business for many years and have spent many of those years learning about why we do the things we do and furthermore, why we don't do many of the things we are capable of doing. Many people are aware that their lives are not all that they had hoped for and would like to change it but very few are aware that they can choose to change it; that its never too late to take action.

I first had the privilege meeting Juan Carlos at an event where I was speaking. He immediately invested in my program demonstrating his commitment to success. In those few minutes I spoke with him, I felt his passion for transforming the world and saw his enthusiasm as he talked about his big dream of sharing what he had learned.

Juan Carlos has been mentored by some of the best in the industry of Personal Growth and Achievement: John C. Maxwell, Bob Proctor, Brian Tracy, Tony Robbins, Brendon Burchard, Wayne Dyer, Deepak Chopra, Dave Ramsey among others.

My passion in life is to train individuals, authors, entrepreneurs, corporate leaders and employees in some of the most compelling and strategic goal-setting technologies of our times. It is my job to help you to realize your success (both mentally, spiritually, and in "the real world"), whatever your chosen field may be! My personal goal is to make a positive contribution to the lives of millions and I am beyond passionate about helping you achieve your goals.

When I decided I needed a change in my life, I looked for help everywhere, every time and with everybody. I couldn't think, focus, or concentrate. I spent years trying different things such as reading, studying, counselling, mentors, seminars, etc. Then I started changing my habits... sometimes succeeding, sometimes failing, but never giving up. I learned that my thoughts were a huge key to the way my mind thinks and processes information. As soon as I began to change my thoughts and my entire way of thinking, my life began to change in a significant way. Things I didn't think I was capable of were suddenly mine for the taking; goals I never thought I could achieve were becoming attainable.

> *"All you need is the plan, the road map,*
> *and the courage to press on to your destination."*
> – Earl Nightingale

Use this book as your road map to making changes in your life that you never thought were possible. Many of us, including myself, come to a point in our lives where we begin to question everything around us. The key is not to dwell on the past but rather take those lessons and apply them to your life today. Embrace your failures as experiences and use them to motivate yourself to do better in the future. To learn how to do this all of this, you simply have to read this book and follow the steps provided.

Juan Carlos provides every reader the tools to change their lives by replacing old habits with new ones; habits that will help you in every area of your life. This is a practical guide that will help you realize your dreams and make them come true. His devotion to helping people and enthusiasm in how he delivers his message is both eye opening and entertaining. The wisdom within these pages will help you discover your true potential and be empowered to act on it.

Throughout the book we are taught that creating habits and being disciplined is the best way to create a lasting and permanent change. You will learn how to find the meaning of your life. This book will not only simplify your life, it will increase your motivation and will teach you that whatever you think about, you give energy to, so you are therefore attracting it into the physical world.

Our lives are not determined by what happens to us but by how we react to what happens; not by what life brings to us, but by the attitude we bring to life. The life changing information and tools within these pages can be used as your guide to understanding yourself and realizing the extraordinary power that is within you. You can have a life filled with anything in the world you desire.

By Peggy McColl, *New York Times* Bestselling Author

Table of Contents

Overview

My Story

From Your MIND – "Thoughts" Logical Perspective (conscious)

    1. Knowing Your <u>Desire</u>: What do you want? "Think BIG"
       Self-Awareness of Your Deepest Desires in All Areas of
       Your Life (Goal Types)
       Purpose (by logic) vs. Passion (by heart)

    2. Doing Your <u>Decision</u>: How do you get it? "Start SMALL"
       Determination: Self Confidence to Quickly Choose and
       Slowly Change
       Discipline: Internal Change - Mental Faculties
       (Think, Be, Do, Have, Give)

From Your HEART – "Feelings" Emotional Perspective (subconscious)

    3. Your <u>Self-Image</u>: Who are you?
       Internal Change Through Positive Affirmations
       External Change Through Emotional Impact

    4. Your <u>Beliefs</u>: What do you believe in?
       Knowledge = Understanding (study) "logic" + faith "feeling"
       Fear vs. Faith (Creator vs. Compete) Acceptance

    5. Your <u>Habits</u>: What do you do?
       Based on Being God Oriented, Growth Oriented, Goal Oriented
       Replacing Paradigms, a Collection of Habits

From Your ACTIONS – "Doing" Behavioral Perspective
(choose from desired feelings)

    6. Habits to SPARK and Generate Your *Motivation*:
       <u>Desire</u> *"internal – conscious"* (ambition)
            To be more, to do more, to have more
       <u>Clarity</u> Development in Four Steps
       <u>Believe</u> *"external – subconscious"* (faith)
            Vision Boards (visual and physical "external" action)
            Visualizations (imagination and mental "internal" action)

7 Habits to SUSTAIN and Maintain Your *Motivation*:

> Focus "*internal – conscious*" (attention)
>> Use your *willpower* to concentrate your thoughts

> Effort "*external – subconscious*" (try, action)
>> Use your movement "automatically" to attempt to gain momentum

8. Habits to AMPLIFY and Grow Your *Motivation*:

> Attitude "*internal – conscious*" (thought + feeling + action)
>> Ability to make a Choice + Good attitude = Good Results
>> Good Attitude in Each Area of Your Life

> Environment "*external*" (Relationships)
>> God (Spiritual, Higher Level)
>> People (Mastermind Groups) Others' Knowledge, Ideas, Contacts

SEVEN PRACTICES TO GAIN FOCUS EVERY DAY

FOCUS ON YOU – TO BE

> 1. *Be Healthier, Wealthier and Happier*
> a. Soul: Prayer, Meditation, Gratitude
> b. Mind: Reading, Writing, Thinking
> c. Heart: Music, Singing, Dancing
> d. Body: Nutrition, Exercise, Resting

FOCUS ON YOU – TO DO

> 2. *Generate Enthusiasm*
> 3. *Face a Fear or Difficulty*
> 4. *Focus on Three Things to Do*

FOCUS ON OTHERS – TO DO

> 5. Act of Kindness
> 6. Be The First To Help
> 7. Surprise People To Show How Much They Matter.
> Leave everyone with the impression of increase

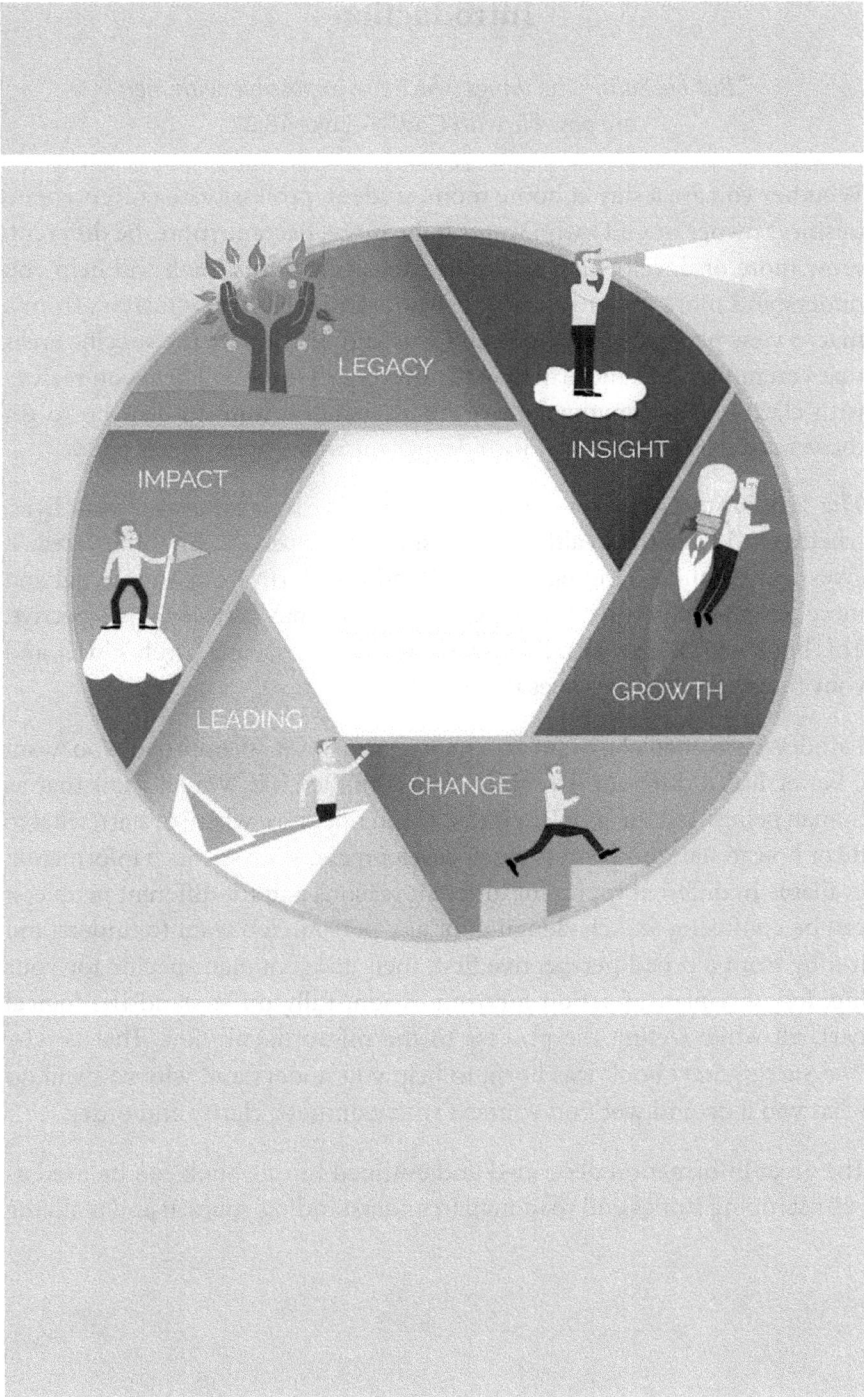

Introduction

"But He Said, 'The things which are impossible with men are possible with God.'" – Luke 18:27

Whether you are a stay at home mom, student, professional, entrepreneur, business owner or CEO who wants to be more, become more, be different, grow more or develop and improve extensively – this book will help you understand more about life, how it works and what really matters from a macro view perspective so you can focus and develop on the specific areas that you might need more help with. This bigger view will help you realize, with clarity, the strengths and weakness that you want to develop to get those results in a better way, with deeper meaning, and a faster pace.

The Success Start gives you the ability to improve in every area of your lives, whether it is health, wealth, relationships, finances, or any other area. It gives you an understanding to change and transform from an internal and more permanent perspective, rather than an external, occasional perspective. This book will change your life, your children's lives, your family's lives, and your future generations' lives if you fully apply it.

I understand that you want to change, you want to improve, you want a better life, a different life, and a more fulfilled life. We all want that as human beings, but the problem is that we do not know where to start, what to do or how to start this process of self development. With so much information available in different topics for different reasons and for different people, it can be confusing and challenging for any person. You want to understand it fully from a broad perspective first, then design a plan specific for your life, follow a plan of action for your vision, fully understand the logical part, all while feeling the process to the micro detail view. That is why *The Success Start* book was born; to help you understand why you will do what you'll do and work on yourself with calmness, clarity and order.

The great information described and outlined in this book can be used as your stepping stones and road map to understanding yourself and realizing the extraordinary power that is within you. You can have a life filled with fun and loving ways, with joy and bliss. You can enjoy a loving, lasting marriage or relationship. You can be wealthy, prosperous and have abundance beyond your wildest dreams and have anything in the world you desire.

If you want your life to be different, you must be different. You must start doing different things to have different things in your life. When you have different things, you will get different results. What is really holding you back from your position at this very moment? What if you could learn to remove that small stone or obstacle that can create a huge shift in your life and your future? Today, you are standing on the edge of a decision and a good choice with clarity, determination, belief, faith and hope. A monumental change and transformation can happen in an instant and yes, it can and it will happen to you.

Today, you are different. You are reading this book. You want to learn. You want to grow. You are searching. You are looking for more. You want to be more. You desire more.

That is great! That is wonderful! Congratulations! I am so proud of you!

Be different. Become different. Decide to be different. Choose to be different.

I believe every human being can do much more than they can actually imagine.

I believe in you. I believe you can. I believe you can do it.
Go for it. Just go for it.
Do it. Just do it.
You can. You can do it. You will do it. Stop thinking about it. Begin today. Start now.
You are ready. You are worthy. You are capable.
We need you. Your family needs you. The world needs you.
Push yourself. Challenge yourself. Encourage yourself.
It is possible. It is worthy. It is here. You are there.
You are important. You are valuable. You are able. You matter.
Be the change you want to see in the world. Become your very best. Become the real you.

Remember that...

Your choices matter. Your decisions matter. Your ideas matter. Your words matter. Your actions matter. You matter. They are powerful. They are meaningful. They are worthwhile.

You are a perfect, original, unique and special creation of God. You are awesome, you are gifted with talents. You are enough.

It is possible to get what you want. It is possible to receive the desires of your heart. It is accessible. It is reachable. It is attainable. Just follow your dreams. Pursue them intentionally, with passion.

Love yourself. Love others. Feel loved. Forgive yourself. Forgive others. Feel forgiveness. Trust yourself. Trust others. Feel trusted. Believe in yourself. Believe in others. Believe it is possible for your dreams to come true and it will be.

MY STORY

Many people over the last three years have asked me, "Juan Carlos, what did you do to become the person you are now? What books did you read? What audios did you listen to? What videos did you watch? What seminars did you go to? Who helped you? Who coached you? Who mentored you? How did you find them? The most often asked question was, "How did you ever get started on the path of Personal Growth?" I tell them that, unfortunately, it grew out of a very negative and painful situation.

I went through a long and painful divorce in 2013. Being a single dad with two children was challenging. I had only two choices: being the same way or change to improve and be a better person. I chose to change. I made a decision to be a better person. I thought about my boys, their future and my children's children. I thought about my own life, that I want to have a wife, to have a family, and the only way to make sure I can be successful in doing so was transforming myself. I decided to change spiritually, to change mentally, to change emotionally and to change physically in all areas of my life.

I decided to be the best dad, the best husband, the best friend, the best businessman, the best Christian. I intentionally look for help everywhere, every time and with everybody.

There was a time in my life when I couldn't think, I couldn't focus, I couldn't concentrate, I couldn't work. I was obese, unhappy and a very stressed person until I realized that I had to change my life after the doctor told me that I could die at anytime. I struggled for several years, trying different things such as diets, exercise, reading, studying, counseling, mentors, seminars, etc. Not only did I spend a lot of money, time and energy but I was looking for a fast solution, a quick fix, a long-term remedy to be a better person. Nothing helped until I put everything together that I had learned into one system, in one way, and began to easily follow it myself.

I tried to master different things in my life, changing habit after habit... trying and trying, failing and failing, giving up and giving up until something clicked in me and made me become more persistent in finding ways to be more effective and efficient, until I discovered new things that continue to work in my life.

YOU CAN DO IT

I believe that we all can do this; you can do it. I believe that this world needs a change, needs progress, and it is ready for this change. People want to change, people want to improve their lives, they just don't have the right system to follow, they don't understand why they must do things to improve their lives, they don't know their other options.

I believe that the earlier you start to implement these habits, rituals, routines or practices, the more you will benefit the rest of your life. The way you think will impact the way you feel, and that will impact your final action.

Have you ever wondered why you do what you do? It's because of your thought patterns, your thoughts, the way your mind thinks and processes information. Those thoughts will make you feel happy or unhappy, positive or negative, right or wrong... and those thoughts will come into the physical form, becoming actions in your personal life.

Imagine if this would happen to you every day... you wake up early, energetic, fully rested, with confidence, feeling happy, feeling love, feeling gratitude, and with a clean mind to start your day.

Imagine if you could change your life today and turn it into a positive pathway, a positive route, a positive way to improve your own life so you could help change other people's lives. Trust me, the feeling of helping other people is greater than anything else you could imagine.

The Success Start gives you tips and strategies, and provides you with sources and tools that I have gathered throughout several years; the ones that made it easy to change my own life. Now I want to share it with YOU, with others, with the world; to make a difference, to make a significant change in this world.

The world is changing. More and more people are becoming obese, are not happy with their work, are getting divorced; crime rates are going up, and more violent people are starting at a young age. With all these trends, the problem is usually the way they were raised, their home lives. The way we wake up in the morning and start our day, in a positive or negative way, will impact the rest of our lives.

This new model to change lives must start in the early morning. Creating habits and being disciplined is the best way to create a lasting and permanent change.

It's possible – you can do it too. I changed my life completely, for the better, even when I thought I was not ready. You are ready now. You can start with a single step today and you will feel and act different tomorrow.

This book will transform your life because it will show you what to do in the mornings to improve your mind, which will make you feel better and, consequently, your actions will improve and your results will be aligned with what you want in life. This book has three sections: Mind, Heart and Body (thoughts, feelings and actions) to help you better understand why certain things, which become habits, must be done in order to improve your thoughts, the first and main step for real change.

Thank you for taking the time to read this book. Thank you for trying and pushing yourself one more time. I know what you are thinking, I know how that feels. I know your frustrations. I have being there many times. But please keep moving and never give up. You are almost there, trust me... it is coming, and it will come the moment you least expect it.

"I WALK slowly, but I never walk BACKWARD."
– Abraham Lincoln

"Because of your faith, it will happen."
– Matthew 9:29b (NLT)

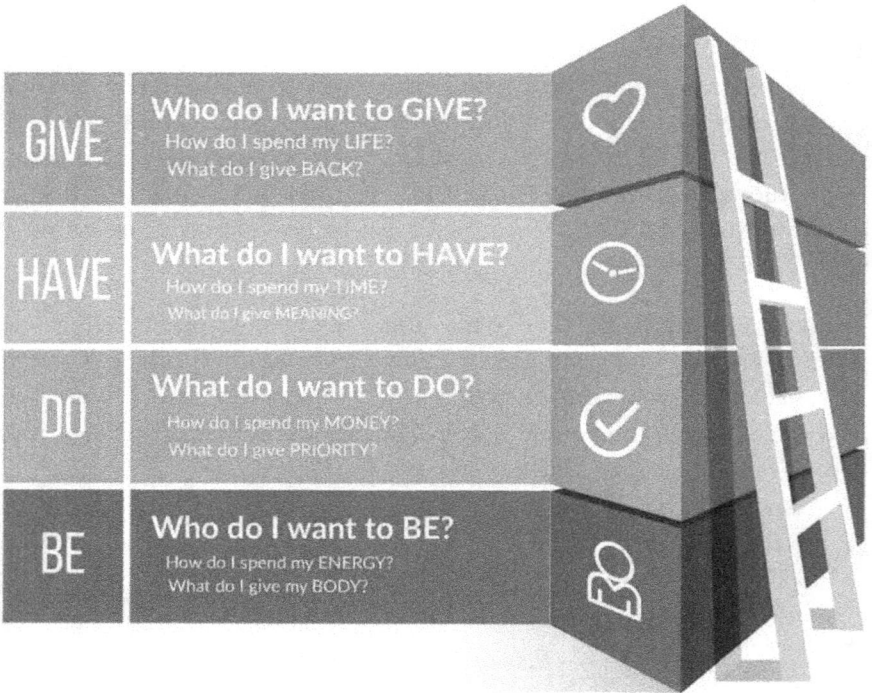

GIVE	Who do I want to GIVE? How do I spend my LIFE? What do I give BACK?	
HAVE	What do I want to HAVE? How do I spend my TIME? What do I give MEANING?	
DO	What do I want to DO? How do I spend my MONEY? What do I give PRIORITY?	
BE	Who do I want to BE? How do I spend my ENERGY? What do I give my BODY?	

1. What Do You REALLY Want?

"You do not have because you do not ask."
– James 4:2

What do you deeply desire in your personal and professional life? What are your big dreams? What are your greatest fantasies? What are your deepest desires? What makes your heart beat faster? What are your authentic aspirations? What are your greatest ambitions? What are you "hungry" for? What are your goals? What is your vision and mission for the future?

What makes you really happy? What makes you sing with joy? What do you laugh about? What makes you have tears of happiness, of bliss? What do you really enjoy doing in life? What wakes you up smiling in the morning? What "more" do you want in life? What do you want to trade the days of your life for? What do you want to do for the rest of your life?

Let's go even deeper to help you think and carefully reflect about some of the most important questions in your life. What do you really want to BE? What do you really want to DO? What do you really want to HAVE? What do you really want to GIVE?

Let's now get a broader understanding to give you more clarity. What areas in your life are the most important to you now and in the future? Is it Health, Love, Spirituality (God), Work (Mission, Charity), Wealth (Finances), Family/Friends (Relationships)?

Let's understand it a little better from different perspectives, the mind and the heart. What is your passion? What do you love to do (the logical - mind perspective)? What is your purpose? What are you gifted to do? What are your talents (the feeling - heart perspective)? Purpose is the reason you journey and why "you do what you do". Passion is the fire and "the spark" that lights your way.

Let's view it from an action and physical world perspective. Who would you like to "be" if you could be anybody? What would you "do" if you knew you couldn't fail? What would you "have" if you could have anything? What would you "give" if you won the lottery? Just imagine that you can have access to all the resources and you can have anything you want in life.

Let's start from the end of mind perspective, one of the best and deepest ways to think and reflect about life, love and what really matters. How would you like to be remembered after you "are" gone? If you had six months to live, what would you "do" first? What legacy do you want to "leave" for your children, your spouse, your family, your friends?

You have to DESIRE something you really want. You must develop self awareness and fully understand how you want to live your life. You have to make a DECISION once you find what you really want. Develop self confidence and be firm on what you decide.

For now, just focus on WHAT you really want now as it will change in the near future as your personal growth develops. Really choose what you WANT without knowing or understanding HOW you are going to get it. This is the secret and the most important part of defining what it is. The WANT must come primarily from your heart, as the HOW always comes from the mind and involves logical understanding.

Why do you want it? This question helps you dig deeper for a meaningful reason. You want to achieve more, be more, give more, have more, for SOMETHING or SOMEBODY. You really want to be, do and have this dream for things greater than yourself. You want change or transform. You want to advance, stretch and grow.

Your why is for something meaningful and valuable, for a mission, cause, goal or dream, to make a difference. Do you want to make an impact on the world? Do you want to leave a legacy? Do you want to contribute to society? Do you want to leave and make a mark for others to follow? Do you want to leave and make a lasting change on humankind?

Is it for somebody else – for your spouse, your children, your parents, your community, your next generation? Do you want to be a better person? A better parent? A better spouse? A better son or daughter?

In other words, the two most important questions in your life will be: WHERE AM I GOING? WHO IS COMING WITH ME?

There are three types of personal and professional goals people set in their lifetimes:

Bad Goals

They are based on KNOWING how to get it. They're based on present results of being, doing or having the same material possessions, just new or upgraded. For example: If you have a job now... your goal is to have another "new" job of the same type.

Ok Goals

They are based on PLANS that are <u>visible</u>. They're usually what you "think" you can do or what you "think" you might need. They have a planning sequence, a step by step process. For example: If you want to have a business now... you know all the steps, strategies and processes to get there, and know exactly how to do it.

Best Goals

They are based on DREAMS that are <u>invisible</u>. You have no idea HOW you are going to get it, but you know deeply that is what you really want. You do not think, you do not worry and you do not have fear of any kind about how the goal is going to be accomplished. Just think of what you WANT, as thinking about the "how" will either limit or destroy the fantasy. That fantasy that might look impossible at first will then become improbable, but finally it will be inevitable.

A few ideas to consider and remember:

Do you really need MOTIVATION if you are going the wrong way?

Do you really need PERSISTANCE if you are doing the wrong goals?

Do you really need RESILIENCE if you are being strong on the wrong goals?

Do you really need FOCUS if you are focusing on the wrong destination?

The difference between a NEED and a WANT

Needs are reactive. You may need something but don't really want it.

Wants are proactive. You may want something but don't really need it.

HOW DO YOU DECIDE WHAT YOU REALLY WANT?

KNOWING what it is that you really want is the first step to living a successful and significant life. Your goal must be big. Dream big. It should excite you (mental – mind level) and scare you (emotional – heart level) at the **same** time. Below are some exercises from four different perspectives, along with techniques that will help you and guide you through the process in a more logical way. Start now.

SPIRITUAL "soul"

1. Pray to God.

2. Have silent time.

3. Put some soft music on in the background.

4. Journal daily; every morning and every evening.

5. Write what you want – your dreams – until you have tears in your eyes.

LOGICAL "wide"

1. List and prioritize important areas in your personal and professional life.

2. List and prioritize goals in each area you described above.

3. List and prioritize short and long terms goals.

EMOTIONAL "deep"

1. Quickly write a list of 30 things you want to BE (write non-stop, everything that comes to mind).

2. Quickly write a list of 30 things you want to DO.

3. Quickly write a list of 30 things you want to HAVE.

4. Quickly write a list of 30 things you want to GIVE.

PHYSICAL "action"

1. Choose one goal, with a date, and write it on a card.

2. Carry it with you at all times for the next 30 days.

3. Read it loud and really feel it twice daily for 30 days.

4. Memorize your goal. Is this what you really want?

5. After 30 days, move on to your next most important goal.

6. In addition, you can create a vision board for your wall that looks like this:

```
┌─────────────────────────────────────────┐
│                                           │
│         My PERSONAL GOAL                  │
│                                           │
│   MY GOAL _____ 20 ___         │
│                                           │
│   I am so happy and grateful now that.... │
│                                           │
│   _____   │
│                                           │
└─────────────────────────────────────────┘
```

BIBLE

"I CAN do all things through Christ who strengthens me."
– Philippians 4:13 NKJV

"Now glory be to God, by His mighty power at work within us is able to do far more than we would ever dare to ask or even dream of – infinitely beyond our highest prayers, desires, thoughts, or hopes."
– Ephesians 3:20 LB

Faith is choosing and believing God's dream for your life. Nothing starts happening in your life until you start dreaming, thinking or visualizing a dream. God gave you the ability to dream, to fantasize, to imagine, to create. Dreaming is an act of faith. Everything you can see in this world started as a dream. Somebody thought about it first, they dreamed it.

I pray to God that He makes you a positive thinker, gives you hope and lets you see the invisible, makes you feel the intangible, and achieve the impossible.

QUOTES

"In absence of clearly-defined Goals, we become strangely loyal to performing daily trivia, until ultimately we become enslaved by it."
– Robert Heinlein

*"Reach high, for stars lie hidden in your soul.
Dream deep, for every dream precedes the goal."*
– Mother Teresa

"What you get by achieving your goals is not as important as what you become by achieving your goals."
– Zig Ziglar

"When you move with PURPOSE, you collide with DESTINY."
– Bertice Berry

*"The meaning of life is to find your gift.
The PURPOSE of life is to give it away."*
– Pablo Picasso

REFLECTIONS

The tragedy in life isn't about NOT reaching your goal.

The tragedy in life is about having NO GOAL TO REACH.

To reach a goal you have NEVER before attained,

you must do things you have NEVER before done.

It's a dream until you write it down, and then it's a goal.

If an egg is broken by an outside force, LIFE ENDS.

If broken by an inside force, LIFE BEGINS.

Great things always begin FROM INSIDE

I am... (with your SOUL)

I know... (with your MIND)

I believe... (with your HEART)

I do... (with your BODY)

Why do you need to know your purpose? It will explain the meaning of your life. It will simplify your life. It will focus your life. It will increase your motivation. It will prepare you for eternity.

What do you
want *to choose* to see?

~~Impossible?~~

break it down and you'll see...

I'm possible!

It's true, nothing is impossible...

The impossible is possible if you want it to be.

	Mind	**Heart**	**Spirit**
Mission Why	Deliver SATISFACTION	Realize ASPIRATION	Practice COMPASSION
Vision What	Profitability	Returnability	Sustainability
Values How	Be BETTER	DIFFERENTIATE	Make a DIFFERENCE

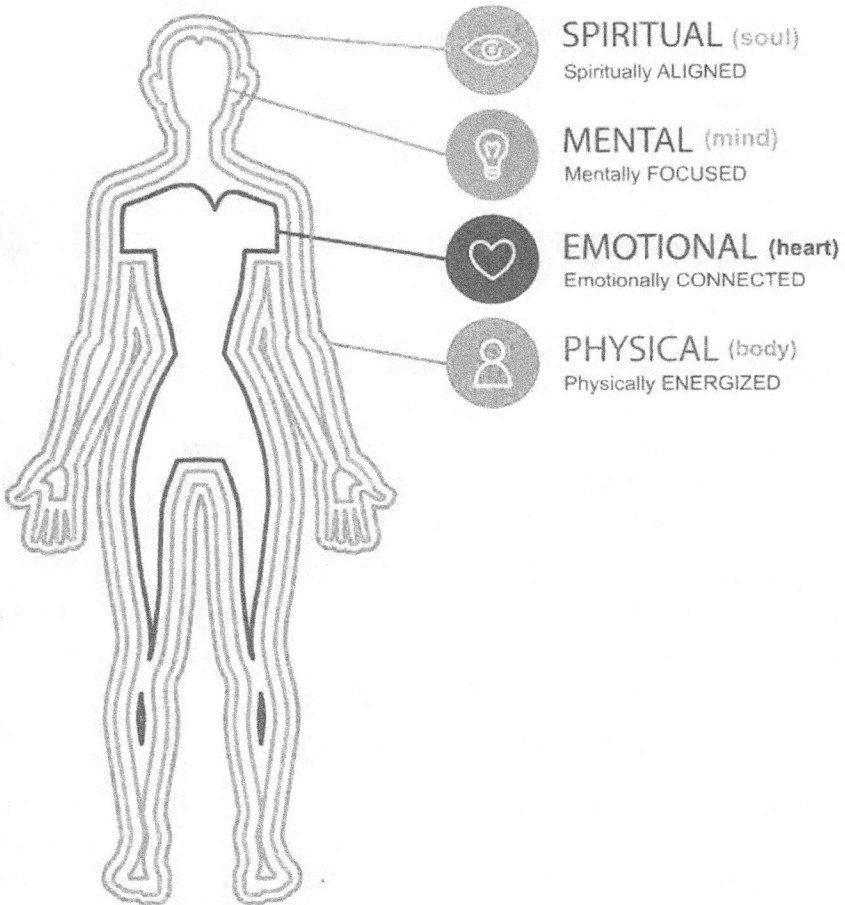

SPIRITUAL (soul)
Spiritually ALIGNED

MENTAL (mind)
Mentally FOCUSED

EMOTIONAL (heart)
Emotionally CONNECTED

PHYSICAL (body)
Physically ENERGIZED

2. How Do You REALLY Get It?

"God has given each of us the ability to do certain things well."
– Romans 12:6a NLT

After finding your DESIRE, having the ability to CHOOSE with self confidence and making a DECISION, you finished with the "knowing" part or the "what" phase and you are ready to start the "doing" part and the "how" phase.

Think and reflect carefully now... if you want something, you want to HAVE it. In order to have it, you must DO something, and in order to do something, you must BE. Therefore, you must first become the person you desire to be – this is the right, logical sequence and only order. Always BE first, before doing and before having.

We cannot GIVE what we do not have. We cannot HAVE what we do not do. We cannot DO if we do not become the best person we can. Be the chance that you want to see in the world. Start with yourself, invest in yourself, change and grow to be your very best.

Change your CIRCUMSTANCES vs. Change YOURSELF

You can think to change your circumstances which are external, outside of you, temporary, usually casually set and lightly taken, or you can think to change yourself which are internal, inside of you, permanent, carefully chosen and firmly taken. There is a big difference between these changes; one can be a small "change" in the same place and the other can be a major "change" or transformation on a whole new level or different place.

Wanting your desire FASTER vs. Wanting your desire FULFILLING

You will get what you want most EASILY if you do that for which you are best FITTED (best talent or skill). However, you will get what you want most SATISFACTORILY if you do that which you really WANT to do. Your real desire to do something is proof that you have within you the power in which to do it. God put that idea in your mind and He will give you the resources to get it done. Remember, doing what you want to do is life... you can always develop any talent as you grow.

Using your six HIGHER MENTAL FACULTIES

On a physical/body level, when we use our five senses to "input" or perceive information directly to us from outside external visible and invisible sources, we use our hands to touch and feel, our mouth to taste and eat, our nose to smell and breath, our ears to hear and listen, and our eyes to look and see.

On a spiritual/soul level we often use prayer, meditation, or quiet time to send and receive "information" to and from God or a Higher Source, including forgiveness for the past, guidance for the future, and wisdom, love, peace, bliss and happiness for the present.

On a mental/mind level we rarely use our six higher mental faculties (which are not visible to the human eye) as often as we use our common five physical senses (touch, taste, smell, hear and see) that was God's gift to us. We were born with them and every single human being in this world has them. These six mental faculties live inside you and they are: imagination, intuition, will, memory, reason and perception.

IMAGINATION

Imagination is the mental faculty or action of forming ideas, images or concepts of external objects not present to the senses. Imagination is the most important one of the mental faculties and the one that unlocks all other higher faculties. Imagination is the ability to allow new images and sensations into your mind. Imagination is an image maker, has no limits and created every innovation, advancement and fortune to many people. Imagine the act, action, goal or result first.

BIBLE

"Do not conform to the pattern of this world, but be transformed by the renewing of your mind. Then you will be able to test and approve what God's will is – his good, pleasing and perfect will."
– Romans 12:2

QUOTES

"Logic will take you from A to B. Imagination will take you <u>everywhere</u>." –
Albert Einstein

"Your imagination is your preview of life's coming attractions."
– Albert Einstein

*"What you THINK, you BECOME. What you FEEL, you ATTRACT.
What you IMAGINE, you <u>CREATE</u>."*
– Buddha

REFLECTIONS

Synthetic imagination is fed by experience, education or observation. It is direct communication to your own and local interaction. It is like the information on your own personal computer. This already exists in the universe.

Creative imagination is fed by God through your ideas, dreams or fantasies. It is a direct communication to infinite intelligence. It is like the information on the whole internet that is worldwide. This does not exist in the universe.

<u>INTUITION</u>

Intuition is an instinct or presentiment. It is the ability to understand something immediately from instinctive feelings, hunches or gut feelings, without the need for conscious reasoning. Intuition is God whispering the answer to you. Intuition is a spiritual faculty and guidance. You talk to God through prayer and God talks back to you through intuition.

BIBLE

*"And after the earthquake a fire; but the Lord was not in the fire,
and after the fire a still small voice."*
– 1 Kings 19:12 KJV

QUOTES

"The only real valuable thing is intuition."
– Albert Einstein

"Intuition is seeing with the soul."
– Dean Koontz

"It is by logic we prove, but by intuition we discover."
– Leonardo Da Vinci

REFLECTIONS

Your subconscious mind communicates to your conscious mind through intuition.

Your intuition is a higher intelligence than logic, it does not explain, it just guides you.

Your subconscious mind communicates to the Universal Mind or Infinitive Intelligence.

<u>WILL</u>

The will is an internal force mental faculty that gives you the ability to focus your attention and concentrate by holding one idea with determination on the screen of your mind, to the exclusion of all outside positive or negative distractions. You can triple your mind power with concentration. Focus gives you powerful leverage over your mind. When you focus on a thought or an idea, it forces your mind to look in the direction of that thought.

BIBLE

"Wisdom is the principal thing; therefore get wisdom:
and with all thy getting get understanding."
– Proverbs 4:7 KJV

QUOTES

"The secret of change is to FOCUS all of your energy, not on
fighting the old, but on building the new."
– Socrates

"People do not lack strength, they lack will."
– Victor Hugo

"Concentration is the roof of all the higher abilities in man."
– Bruce Lee

REFLECTIONS

Meditation will EMPTY and clean the mind when you relax.

Concentration will FILL and add to your mind when you focus.

The will is what you think of as sustained concentration. Whatever you concentrate on, you think about, that is what you will become.

MEMORY

Memory, recollection or remembrance is the mental faculty by which the mind stores and remembers information. You have a perfect memory; everybody has a perfect memory. Memory is developed by ridiculous association and you usually use different techniques to expand and grow your memory.

BIBLE

"But the Comforter, [which is] the Holy Ghost, whom the Father will send in My name, He shall teach you all things, and bring all things to your remembrance, whatsoever I have said unto you."
– John 14:26 KJV

QUOTES

"Memory is deceptive because it is colored by today's events."
– Albert Einstein

"Memory is the mother of all wisdom."
– Awschylus

"The true art of memory is the art of attention."
– Samuel Johnson

REASON

Reason is the mental faculty that has the power of the mind to think, reflect, understand and form judgments by a process of logic. You can learn to think just as you learn a foreign language or to play a piano. You become what you think about. Start thinking with a small picture, then put them together with other pictures in your mind.

BIBLE

"Be careful what you think, because your thoughts run your life."
– Proverbs 4:23

QUOTES

"Faith is a higher faculty than reason."
– H C Bailey

"Faith begins where reason sinks exhausted."
– Albert Pike

*"We can let circumstances rule us, or we can take charge
and rule our lives from within."*
– Earl Nightingale

REFLECTIONS

There is no such thing as a bad memory, only a weak memory. You have a perfect memory, so be aware of it.

Remember to use your memory carefully and that your body changes the vibration (feeling or emotions) when you speak, so make sure it is positive.

PERCEPTION

Perception is a mental faculty that gives you the ability to see, hear or become aware of something through the senses. Your perception is your point of view and you depend on that point of view. You use it all the time but you must be able to make a shift to be able to find new ideas, new visions or new opportunities. You can have anything you want to have but you must first change the way you look at your life.

BIBLE

*"Finally, brothers and sisters, whatever is true, whatever is noble,
whatever is right, whatever is pure, whatever is lovely,
whatever is admirable – if anything is excellent or praiseworthy –
think about such things."*
– Philippians 4:8

QUOTES

"We can complain because rose bushes have thorns, or rejoice because thorn bushes have roses."
– Abraham Lincoln

"We don't see things as they are, we see things as we are."
– Anais Nin

"There is no truth. There is only perception."
– Gustave Flaubert

REFLECTIONS

1. Goal

2. Dream

3. Passion

4. Purpose

Follow a DREAM to find a PASSION, follow your passion as it will lead you to your PURPOSE.

There is no right or wrong way of doing anything, But there is always a better way to think or do something.

Perception through PLACE (by moving) ideas or sources within – Inside the location, or external – outside the location.

Perception through PEOPLE (by asking) within your contacts, people outside your contacts, or strangers.

Perception through VIEW (by seeing) as a bug's view (same level) or God's view (rise above it).

QUESTIONS TO REFLECT ON AND THINK ABOUT

Why did you become what you ARE?

Why do you do what you DO?

Why do you have what you HAVE?

Why do you give what you GIVE?

Immature

COMPETE,

Professionals

CREATE

3. Self-Image

"The Apostle Paul said, '...but this one thing I do: forgetting what lies behind and reaching forward to what lies ahead."
– Romans 12:6a NLT

Who You Are

Your self-image, personal values and self-awareness, both positive and negative, affect you and your subconscious mind mainly from three different sources – your parents, people you interact with, and what you tell yourself.

You inherited certain personal values, like your self-image, beliefs and ideas from your parents when you were born, and developed as a child. Those ideas, beliefs and values created your self-image and affected your self confidence and self esteem from a very early age.

You interacted with people at work, with your boss, your friends, your colleagues; at your school through your classmates, teachers and coaches; in your community through church priests, pastors, leaders, judges, politicians; and even through mass media including TV, movies, internet, newspapers, magazines, and many others.

You, yourself, intentionally or unintentionally, think, speak or write sentences, statements, affirmation or declarations without a conscious awareness of what you are doing, why you are doing it, how you are doing it, and even when you are doing it.

Some positive statements created and shaped your self-image in a positive way, which is the reason you have positive values, beliefs, ideas and thoughts. At the same time, through a universal law of Polarity, some negative statements also created and shaped your self-image in a negative way and that is the reason you have negative values, beliefs, ideas and thoughts.

Just to be clear, the universal law of Polarity is as real and important as the universal law of Gravity; whether you believe it or not, it does exist. The law of Polarity states that for every positive there must be a negative; in other words everything must have an opposite in this world.

Now that you understand that you have, within yourself, both positive and negative values, ideas and beliefs that created your self-image until now – at this very moment – you can change it, you can modify it, and you can improve it using several techniques. You will first clean the "area", your subconscious mind, and then plant the new and improved positive ideas, beliefs and values that you choose to create a better self-image, a better you; the very best person you want to become.

You can "clean and clear" your mind through Meditation practices, Quiet Time, Praying to God, Contemplation and Solitude. Connect yourself with mother nature; go to the beach, to a park, get sun, get in the rain, be yourself, be alone; no music, no phone, no interruptions... just be you. Be quiet, be calm and try not to think about anything. As you know, we live in a world full of chaos, distractions, fears and frustrations, and it could be very hard to focus on you.

Only after you clean or clear your mind for that moment – on a conscious level – can you start "adding" or changing your mind – on a subconscious level – to a new you, to new ideas and to new beliefs. Then your self-image will improve.

There are only two ways to change your subconscious mind. One is through a big, emotional impact such as the 9/11 Terrorist Attack in the U.S., which is usually negative in nature, and the other one used by many people is by using a constant repetition of affirmations.

Now, the repetition of affirmations must be done at a minimum, preferably as soon as you wake up in the morning and right before you go to bed, for a minimum of 30 days. This can be done using any combination of your senses, including speaking, writing, listening or seeing. The most effective ones are the ones where you speak the affirmation with EMOTION in your heart, forcing you to feel it, and the one where you write the affirmation with THOUGHTS in your mind, forcing you to think about them.

Remember that when you change your ideas, you change your beliefs and your personal values, which changes your overall self-image, and improves your self-confidence and self-esteem. Once your self-image is "higher", stronger and more positive, then and only then, will you be able to set the "right" goals; your habits and your actions to get the results you want for your life.

You can set positive affirmations and view them from this perspective as being much more effective. When you set your affirmations for your personal values and beliefs, those affirmations will give you a better self-image, a better you and your <u>heart</u> (feelings) – subconscious mind. When you set the affirmations for your goals, those affirmations will provide focus and clarity to you and your <u>mind</u>. When you set your affirmations for your habits and actions, those affirmations will provide encouragement and inspiration to your <u>actions</u>.

Benefits of Positive Affirmations

1. Increase, Raise and Improve your Self-Awareness

2. Increase, Raise and Improve your Self-Confidence

3. Increase, Raise and Improve your Self-Esteem

4. Increase, Raise and Improve your Self-Worth

5. Increase Raise and Improve, your Self-Image

Affirmations to Have Joy, Bliss and Happiness

Happiness comes from the growth, the progress and fulfillment, not the achievement of certain actions we do on the spiritual, mental, emotional and physical levels; happiness is a process, not a destination. In other words when you think, you feel. When you feel, you act. When you take action, you see results and become what you desire to be. When you are the person you want to be, then you can do. When you can do, then you can have. When you can have, then you can give.

1. <u>Gratefulness</u> on a Spiritual Level (to make a difference)

Be grateful for your PAST: Forgive – Makes sense of the past

Be grateful for your PRESENT: Feel – Brings peace

Be grateful for your FUTURE: Clarity – Creates vision

2. Memories on a Mind Level (to be better)

  Create a moment, create a memory

3. Experiences on a Heart Level (to do and differentiate)

  Create excitement, create an experience

4. Material Things on a Physical Level (to have different things)

Types of Positive Affirmations

FOR YOUR THOUGHTS" mind" (Your Self-Image)
Values – "I am..."

I am loved. I am loveable. I am surrounded by love.

I am the best.

To build **SELF WORTH** (Self Esteem Affirmations)

  I like myself

  I can do it.

  I can do anything. I know...

Beliefs – "I believe..."
YOU

I believe in myself. I am in control of my attitude.

I believe that something wonderful is going to happen to me today.

I have been selected by God to do...

LIFE

My life is filled with love. My life is abundant in every way.

FOR YOUR EMOTIONS "heart" (Your Goals)
Gratefulness - "I feel..."

I am grateful for my life. I am so happy and grateful for my health.

Actions – "I do..."

I am happily resting inside my brand new dream home by the ocean.
I am feeling love by walking on the beach with my loving spouse and children.
Do it now!

**FOR YOUR ACTIONS "physical body" (Your)
Habits - "I have..."**

I wake up at 6:00 a.m. every day to exercise.

Goals - "I give..."

I give to others unconditional love.

I am the first to help others.

From Thinking (Thoughts) to Actions (Results)

THINKING IMPROVES

When you are quiet and restful, your self-awareness improves,

When your self-awareness improves, your clarity improves,

When your clarity improves, your THOUGHTS improve,

When your thoughts improve, your BELIEFS improve,

When your beliefs improve, your personal VALUES improve.

FEELINGS IMPROVE

When your values improve, your DESIRES improve,

When your desires improve, your DECISION making improves,

When your decision making improves, your self-confidence improves.

When your self-confidence improves, your self-esteem improves,

When your self-esteem improves, your self-image improves,

When your self-image improves, your self-worth improves.

ACTIONS IMPROVE

When your self-worth improves, your attitude improves,

When your attitude changes, your behavior improves,

When your behavior changes, your actions improve,

When your actions improve, your habits improve,

When your habits improve, your character improves,

When your habits improve, your results improve,

When your results improve, you BECOME better,

When you become better, you can DO better,

When you can do better, you can HAVE more,

When you can have more, you can GIVE more.

Positive Affirmations

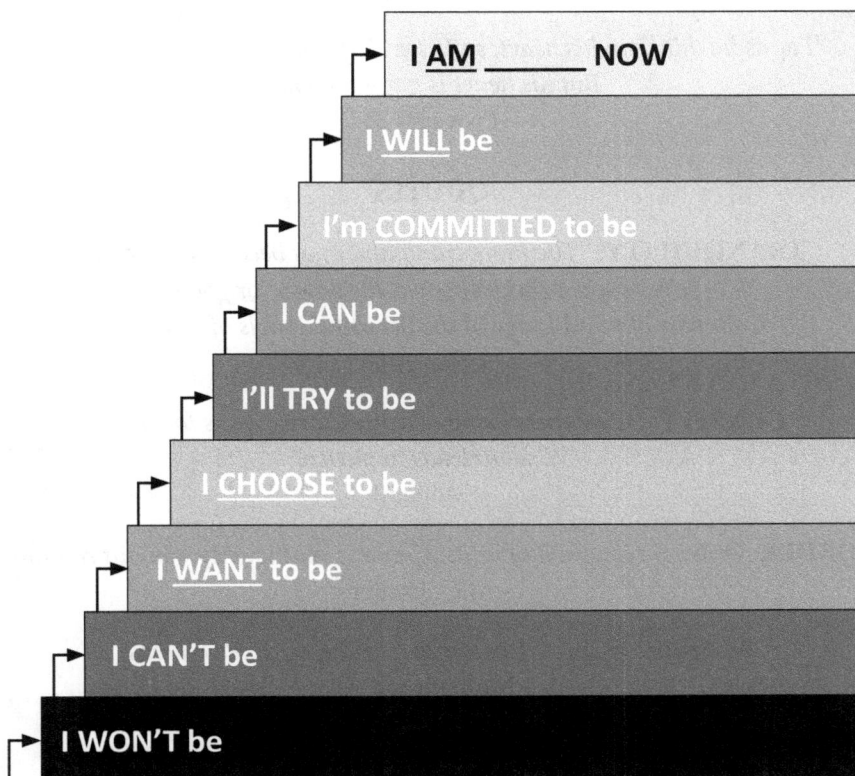

I AM _____ NOW

I WILL be

I'm COMMITTED to be

I CAN be

I'll TRY to be

I CHOOSE to be

I WANT to be

I CAN'T be

I WON'T be

BIBLE

*"Do not conform to the pattern of this world, but be transformed by
the renewing of your mind. Then you will be able to test and approve what
God's will is – his good, pleasing and perfect will."*
– Romans 12:2 NIV

*"Do not be anxious about anything, but in every situation,
through prayer and petition, with thanksgiving, present your requests
to God. And the peace of God, which transcends all understanding,
will guard your hearts and minds in Christ Jesus."*
– Philippians 4:6-7

*"Then you will understand what is right and just and fair,
every good path. For wisdom will enter your heart, and knowledge
will be pleasant to your soul."*
– Proverbs 2:9-10

*"For as he thinks in his heart, so IS he. 'Eat and drink!' he says to you,
But his heart is not with you."*
– Proverbs 23:7

QUOTES

TRANQUILITY: *"The more tranquil a man becomes, the greater
is his success, his influence, his power for good.
Calmness of mind is one of the beautiful jewels of wisdom."*
– James Allen

CLARITY: *"Awareness brings clarity. Clarity leads to wisdom.
Wisdom leads to purity."*
– Mohanji

ORDER: *Order is repetition of units. Chaos is multiplicity without rhythm.*
– M.C. Escher

"'I am the greatest.' I said that even before I knew I was."
– Muhammad Ali

*"Two things that will define you. Your determination when you
have nothing. Your ATTITUDE when you have everything."*
– Unknown

"CHARACTER is how you treat those who can do nothing for you."
– Unknown

REFLECTIONS

Why do people not succeed? It is never because of lack of money, time, contacts, technology or anything in the physical external conscious level, but because of the lack of creativity, decisiveness, passion, honesty, love, and beliefs that are in the emotional internal subconscious level.

Any positive or negative ideas or thoughts from your thinking mind will grow. You can grow "flowers" – HAPPINESS – or you can grow "weeds" – FEAR – in your mind "soil".

You will "attract" your thoughts. Whatever you think about, you give energy to it and, therefore, are attracting it into the physical world.

Thoughts + Emotions = Results (YOUR REALITY)

The image you hold of yourself controls your life.

How do you change your self image? Choose the kind of person you want to be. Ask yourself to think and reflect... *Who do I really want to be?*

When your soul is in charge of your ego, everything "flowers" – feels right.

When your ego is in charge of your soul, everything will be "harder" later, and feels hard now.

Make the

REST

of Your Life

The

BEST

of Your Life

4. Believe

"Good things come to those who WAIT, better things come to those who don't GIVE UP, and the best things come to those who just BELIEVE."
– Unknown

What do you believe in?

Several ideas came to you through your ears or sight (input sources) and entered into your mind through external sources (people and interactions), and internal sources (imagination thru thinking) which altered your belief system. As explained before, your beliefs created your self-image up to today. You can change your beliefs and improve your self-image.

How? Read the Bible, read books, read inspirational quotes, speak positive things, help others, encourage others, remove all negativity from your life including news, negative people, etc. Remember, your beliefs will create your facts.

Why? Why does it really matter what I believe or not believe in? Why is it that important or even relevant to this area? The answer is very simple... you will only reach up to what you believe. Whatever you believe becomes your reality. "I am educated." "I believe..." Beliefs are learned, you are not born with them. Question your limiting beliefs. In other words, if you want to reach higher in life in certain areas, you must first start by changing your belief system. What do you really believe you can do?

Believe that you can THINK more.

Believe that you can BE more.

Believe that you can DO more.

Believe that you can HAVE more.

Believe that you can GIVE more.

"Commit to the Lord whatever you do, and your plans will succeed."
– Proverbs 16:3

Am I able to do this? You have infinite potential.

Am I willing to do it? You have to pay the price.

Acceptance and Complaining

Acceptance means that you accept certain things the way they are and you dealt with it already, freeing your mind from negativity, confusion and complaints. When you free and clear your mind, you are ready and able to "input" new ideas, new beliefs, new information, and clarity will emerge. There are three main areas for acceptance which include accepting yourself, accepting your past, and accepting things that you can and cannot control.

Accept Yourself – Be

Accept who you really are. You were born with certain talents and abilities for a purpose. Your dreams will lead you to your passion and your passion will lead you to your purpose. You inherited certain genes from your parents and ancestors, and that DNA helped make you into the person you are. You cannot go back and change it; therefore, just accept it.

Accept the Past – Have

Accept your past. It is over, it is gone and you cannot do anything about it. Your past could have been bad, hurtful and very negative. Bringing memories back to the present time will only hurt you more, influence your mind, and cause you to live negatively. Challenge yourself to think positive, to think another topic and to be able to train your mind to switch those thoughts as soon as they come to you.

Accept Can and Cannot – Do

Accept what you can and cannot do in society and the world. You have to accept the laws, the courts, the politicians... whether you like it or not. Don't waste your time giving negative talks, negative feelings and even reading negative news. Remember to clear your mind from negativity and you will be ready to accept new beliefs into your more positive mind.

Stop Complaints About You

Stop complaining about you, about what you've done, about what you've not done, about why you did what you did, about how you did it, about when you did it. Complaining about you is greatly hurting yourself. Never talk negative to yourself and remember, you are listening yourself. It is entering into your mind and you will believe it later on.

> *"A soft answer turns away wrath, but a harsh word stirs up anger."*
> – Proverbs 15:1

Stop Complaints About Others

Treat other people with respect and never, ever complain about others. Not only are you are speaking negative words but they are receiving negative words from you. Whatever you give, you will get back. If you send negativity, you will get negativity. Always speak positive words, words of encourage-ment, words of motivation or words of inspiration.

You are a Creator

You are here in this world to create. God is the creator of the universe and He made you as His image. God is in you, with you and works through you. If God is a creator, you have the ability to create. He created you. You have to choose to receive knowledge and He will open the door and give you wisdom.

Knowledge through UNDERSTANDING (study) in the conscious level

You receive knowledge through understanding what you study at school, in lectures, books and programs, among many other sources, in the conscious level. This knowledge through understanding is LIMITED to what you can do yourself, what you can input into you and your mind from a specific source at specific times.

Knowledge through FAITH in the subconscious level

You get those ideas, those dreams out of nowhere. Intuition comes to you from different places at different times. Your mind, when it is clean and clear, will be able to be open to God, to the truth, to the Universal Intelligence. This knowledge is UNLIMITED and you will have access to all the knowledge of the Universe through God. Remember, the internet was already here 500 years ago, it's just that somebody "found it" and was aware of its presence. The same thing happened when airplanes were invented. Those brothers who created the planes and discovered a way to fly in the air were just more aware and, through faith, did it. But the ability to have planes and be able to fly in the skies was always here in this universe.

Visualizations

Doing visualizations will help you see, dream and believe, even more, in your desires for your life. In the visual physical world you can actually see your dreams with your physical eyes through pictures. In the non visual, spiritual world, you can actually imagine it with your mind through your thoughts.

In the Visible – Physical World

In the physical world you can use Vision Boards, Vision Movies or Vision Books. Vision Boards, also called Goal Boards or Dream Boards, are pictures of what you desire in all the important areas of your life. Pictures of the future, things you already accomplished, along with some titles and inspirational words. Vision movies are those same pictures with inspirational words but you can add some soft background music and inspiring video to ignite the feeling into your desires. Vision Books are a collection of your goals to accomplish in a lifetime in a sequential order without being displayed all at once on a big wall, as is the case of Vision Boards.

On the Invisible – Spiritual World

This is a little bit more challenging but much more effective for your mind. You use your mind and imagination to feel and experience your goal. The more real you can imagine and visualize it using all of your physical senses, the more you will attract it to your life.

Practice Visualization

1. Be QUIET, inhale a deep breath, close your eyes, and relax.

2. Create a picture of your heart's desires in your mind through your imagination. See the image in color with as many details as possible. Get CLARITY: The more vivid and clear your thoughts, the faster you'll attract and eventually receive it.

3. <u>Hold</u> the picture or image of increase and advancement on the screen of your mind. The longer you can hold your thought (through concentration, focus and willpower), the better. DURATION is important.

4. See and actually feel how happy, wealthy and healthy you look. See yourself in the image as if it is happening this very moment. The amount of INTENSITY and using all of your senses to experience and feel all the enthusiasm is the key. Let that image INSPIRE, FILL and PERMEATE every action, including doing everything you can to be a blessing to others.

5. Have EXPECTANCY, develop your faith, and actualize that your vision will happen. Be calm, positive and patient.

Fear vs. Faith

Fear and Faith are feelings. You cannot see, you cannot touch, you cannot hear them. Feeling is just another word for the conscious awareness of the "vibration" you are in at the present moment. If you have a negative vibration, you will experience a negative feeling and if you have a positive vibration, you will experience a positive feeling.

The opposite of fear is faith. Fear is one of the most destructive emotions there is. When doubt and worry are caused by wrong thinking in your conscious mind, fear automatically enters into your subconscious mind, and instantly your body reacts with anxiety shown in the physical form.

To better understand this, let's go back to the main source and a previous step. When you lack knowledge (either through understanding on a conscious level or through faith on the subconscious level), ignorance arises, and when that happens, your doubts and worry emerges.

So how do you fight fear? With Faith. But how can it be done with Faith? By being grateful, and by looking at life and yourself in a positive way; by being grateful for who you are today, for what you do, for what you have, including for who you were in the past, what you did in the past and what you had in the past. See the beauty in life and everything will shift in a positive way.

TYPES OF FEAR

Fear of LOSS

The fear that you will lose something valuable.

More positive will be... What am I going to gain?

Fear of PROCESS

The fear that the process will be hard and hurtful.

More positive will be... What if I enjoy the process?

"Stay alert, with your eyes wide open in gratitude."
– Col. 4:2

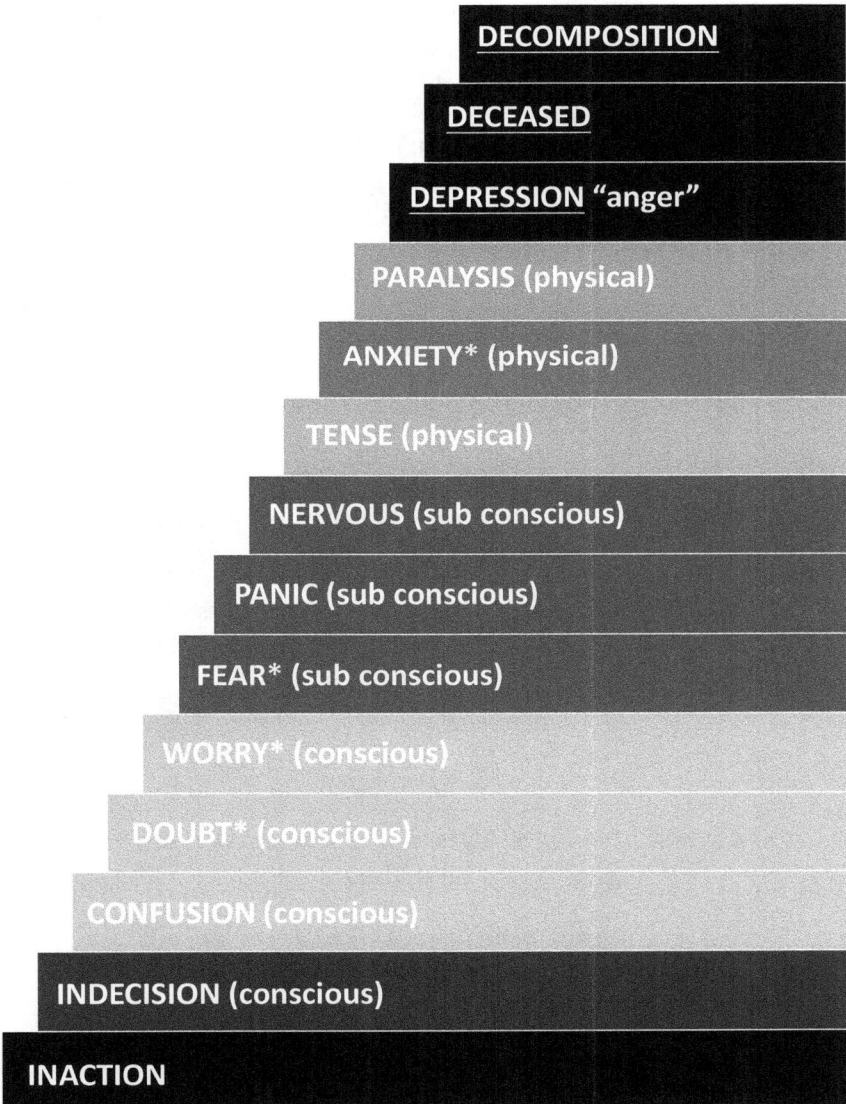

INACTIONS

DECOMPOSITION
DECEASED
DEPRESSION "anger"
PARALYSIS (physical)
ANXIETY* (physical)
TENSE (physical)
NERVOUS (sub conscious)
PANIC (sub conscious)
FEAR* (sub conscious)
WORRY* (conscious)
DOUBT* (conscious)
CONFUSION (conscious)
INDECISION (conscious)
INACTION

BIBLE

"Show me your ways, Lord, teach me your paths.
Guide me in your truth and teach me, for you are God my Savior,
and my hope is in you all day long."
– Psalm 25:4-5

"The wisdom that comes from heaven is first of all pure; then peace loving,
considerate, submissive, full of mercy and good fruit, impartial and sincere."
– James 3:17

"I have made you and I will carry you;
I will sustain you and I will rescue you."
– Isaiah 46:4 NIV

QUOTES

"The opposite of WORRY is trust. Choose to trust God
because you can't change anything by worrying!
– Victoria Osteen

"The greatest mistake you can make in life is to be
continually FEARING you will make one."
– Elbert Hubbard

"We must travel in the direction of our FEAR."
– John Berryman

"You have to step out in FAITH even when you are vibrating in FEAR."
– Bill Hybels

"FEAR is temporary, REGRET is forever."
– Unknown

"Making a big life change is pretty scary.
But, know what's even scarier? REGRET."
– Unknown

"In the end, we only REGRET the chances we didn't TAKE."
– Anonymous

"The bossy may be rich in wealth and intellect,
but the HUMBLE are richer in heart and spirit."
– Unknown

REFLECTIONS

What happens when you cut yourself? Your finger may bleed for a few seconds or minutes, and then heals itself. The healing power is within you, so believe in yourself.

What has fear cost you in your life?

The more you understand you, the more you will believe.

The INTENTION is nice but INITIATIVE (action) is necessary.

Fear is just bad management of your mind.

You defeat fear by your conscious, positive thoughts and disciplined habits.

Are you wishing and hoping OR are you believing and expecting?

Believe it can be done. Demand abundance and prosperity. It takes no more effort to believe the highest.

A group becomes a team when each one BELIEVES.

Turning
NO
to
ON

5. HABITS

"Delight yourself in the Lord; and He will give you the desires of your heart."
— Psalm 37:4

The ACTIONS that you perform regularly or on a daily basis become certain BEHAVIORS that you develop through time, and those behaviors eventually become habits. Habits are developed in your subconscious mind. You do them automatically without thinking about it. Those habits can be positive or negative and the combination, group or multitude of those habits become PARADIGMS.

Therefore, the key is to understand how your habits and paradigms are programmed in your subconscious mind and how to change those "settings" in your mind to what you want to DO.

Similar to changing your SELF-IMAGE through your subconscious mind to what you want to BE, you can also change your HABITS through your subconscious mind to what you want to DO.

As detailed before, there are only two ways to change your subconscious mind. One is through a big emotional impact, which is usually negative in nature, and the other one used by more people is by constant repetition of affirmations through speaking, writing, reading or visualizing.

When you change your paradigms, you change your behavior, and as a consequence your results will also change. So begin at the root of the problem, at the original cause of the problem, and start changing those habits.

Paradigms

Paradigms direct your life and dictate your logic. It controls your logic, and when you change your habits, you change your life.

Paradigms control your behavior and thus your results. Create habits that will lead you to more positive results. You need to change only one or two habits at a time for thirty days.

So how do you do it effectively? First, you have to remove those habits and then you have to create new positive and desirable habits. Write a list of all of your negative habits on a piece of paper, and then burn it. This is a symbolic sign for your mind to recall and remember. You then write your new habit on a piece of paper 100 times in the morning and 100 times in the evening. This is a type of affirmation for your subconscious mind to follow and recall through writing, which will force you to think every single time you write it. In addition, you can record your own voice, speaking loud and clear, stating your new positive habit, then listen to it often throughout the day.

Behavior

Your behavior will change according to your paradigms. Remember, there are two ways to change your paradigms. One is through internal change and inner work as described above. You will be changing your own subconscious mind due to your own efforts through affirmations by writing, speaking or seeing. This inside work is a much stronger and better way for lasting change.

However, there is also a way to change your paradigms or habits due to external change and outer work through your environment. Not only the places you are in but also the people you are surrounded with. Your friends have a tremendous influence on you, in your life and in your future.

If you have an affirmation saying, "I am so happy and grateful that I am working out every day" through your internal work and self-talk, but you have a friend who tells you, "Let's go eat. You look great and don't need to exercise." This friend is putting ideas in your mind that you look great from his perspective and not yours. This will make you think and doubt, forcing you to use your will to be stronger, requiring you to use much more effort in order to continue.

Results

Your paradigms change your behavior, and your behavior changes your results. Think and reflect now about those results. Those results will become you, your legacy. Are those what you REALLY want as described above? Is that what you really desire?

You can use four different ways to have a clear picture of the results you want, to make a better, more logical decision, and to help you think and improve the quality of your life.

1. Be MORE of a certain way (gives you more satisfaction).

2. Be LESS of a certain way (reduce/discontinue).

3. START being the way that you are not currently being (pick new choices).

4. STOP being the way that you are being (evaluate your life with a new perspective).

BIBLE

"Let us not become weary in doing good, for at the proper time we will REAP a HARVEST if we do not give up."
– Galatians 6:9

"The plans of the diligent lead surely to abundance, but everyone who is hasty comes only to poverty."
– Proverbs 21:5 ESV

"GENTLENESS, and SELF-CONTROL. There is no law against these things!"
– Galatians 5:22-23 NLT

"I pray the Lord will guide you to be as loving as God and as patient as Christ."
– 2 Thessalonians 3:5 CEV

QUOTES

"We are what we repeatedly do. Excellence then, is not an act, but a HABIT."
– Aristotle

"Keep your HABITS positive because your habits become your values. Keep your VALUES positive because your values become your destiny."
– Mahatma Gandhi

"ATTITUDE is a reflection of CHARACTER and CHARACTER is a reflection of HABIT."
– Zig Ziglar

"It's never too late to redefine self-control, to change long ingrained habits, and to do the work you're capable of."
– Seth Godin

REFLECTIONS

Bad Habits are much easier to abandon today than tomorrow.

Never allow waiting to become a HABIT. Live your dreams and take risks. Life is happening NOW. IF THERE IS NO WAY, CREATE ONE... make that a habit.

The best makeup is your SMILE. The best jewel is your HUMILITY. The best cloth is your ATTITUDE. The best medicine is to LOVE.

GOD Oriented by Principles	GROWTH Oriented Daily Learning	GOAL Oriented Results and Time
Give the First **PART** of Your Day	**MINDSET** *Will this help me grow?*	**CLARIFY** **Your Purpose**
Give First **PRIORITY** to **Every Decision**	**ACTION** Slowly, Constantly	**DISCOVER** **Your Purpose**
Give First **PLACE** in Your Heart	**SYSTEM** Analysis, Process	**VISUALIZE** **Your Purpose**

Juan Carlos Arzola

DON'T
QUIT

6. SPARK Actions – Start

"Commit your work to the Lord and your plans will be established."
– Proverbs 16:3

How do you start to generate motivation for your actions? How do you begin with the desire to engage and do something? How do you get initially involved and encouraged in that behavior that you really want to do? You have to have a CLEAR and committed mind and BELIEVE with faith that it is possible to develop high levels of motivation.

SPARKING Motivation = DESIRE (Ambition) + BELIEF (Expectancy)

Ambition

Ambition is an even higher level of desire. It is what you want to be, what you want to do, what you want to have, and what you want to give in life. It is the reason, the "why" you want to do it, the logical conscious explanation for doing so. You have to keep clarity in your mind. A clear mind is a healthy mind that is free from negativity, a consciously directed positive mind.

Novelty

The introduction of new experiences, new learning, new events, new goals, new things, new ideas, new places, new people will spark and activate the drive to push yourself to those required actions. Your desires and ambitions to add MORE novelty in life is one of the main drives that pushes us humans to advance.

Expectancy

To believe is it possible, to have faith that it will happen, and to expect it to come, comes from the subconscious mind. You have to feel it deeply in your heart. You must even act as if you already have what you really want. Your positive attitude toward your thoughts, feelings and actions will determine your drive.

You have to learn to choose to act and walk by faith, not feelings. Faith is not a feeling, faith is an action.

> *"FAITH is like WI-FI, it's invisible but it has the power to CONNECT you to what you need."*
> – Unknown

> *"When fear enters your MIND, flip the switch and choose FAITH. After all, both fear and faith demand you believe in something you cannot see. Affirmation: my fears are melting away."*
> – Bob Proctor

> *"I wait expectantly, trusting God to help, for He has promised."*
> – Psalm 130:5 TLB

DEVELOPING YOUR BEHAVIOR

You must have a plan to develop routines to bring your own motivation yourself as nobody will bring it to you. You must generate motivation from within. But why? How? You create those habits to make them "automatically" (subconscious mind) and you can keep and have permanent change in your thoughts, feelings and actions. You must begin with tactics to start – spark the motivation itself to get each habit accomplished.

4 PHASES OF CHANGE

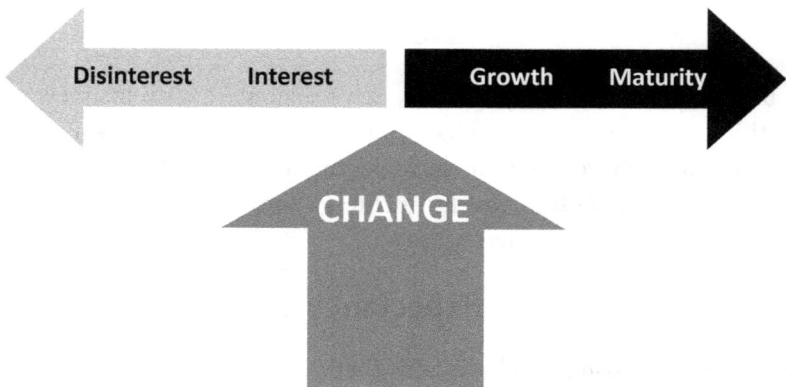

Disinterest   Interest   Growth   Maturity

CHANGE

BIBLE

*"Do not be afraid or discouraged. Go out there tomorrow,
for the Lord is with you!"*
– JOSHUA 1:9

*"Ask and it will be given to you; Seek and you will find; Knock and the door
will be opened to you. For everyone who asks receives; he who seeks finds;
and to him who knocks, the door will be opened.*
– MATTHEW 7:7-8

*"Enter through the narrow gate. For wide is the gate and broad is the road
that leads to destruction, and many enter through it. But small is the gate
and narrow the road that leads to life, and only a few find it."*
– Matthew 7:13-14

QUOTES

*"A great ATTITUDE becomes a great mood, which becomes a great day,
which becomes a great year, which becomes a great life."*
– Zig Ziglar

*"Two Thing Define You: Your PATIENCE when you have NOTHING.
Your ATTITUDE when you have EVERYTHING."*
– Imam Ali

*"The greatest of human emotions is LOVE. The most valuable of human
gifts is the ability to LEARN. Therefore, learn to love."*
– UJ Ramdas

*"Everyone THINKS of changing the world, but no one
thinks of CHANGING himself."*
– Leo

REFLECTIONS

Our lives are not determined by what happens to us but by how we react to
what happens; not by what life brings to us, but by the attitude we bring to life.

The opposite of courage is conformity.

The plan can change. The goal cannot change.

START – BABY STEPS

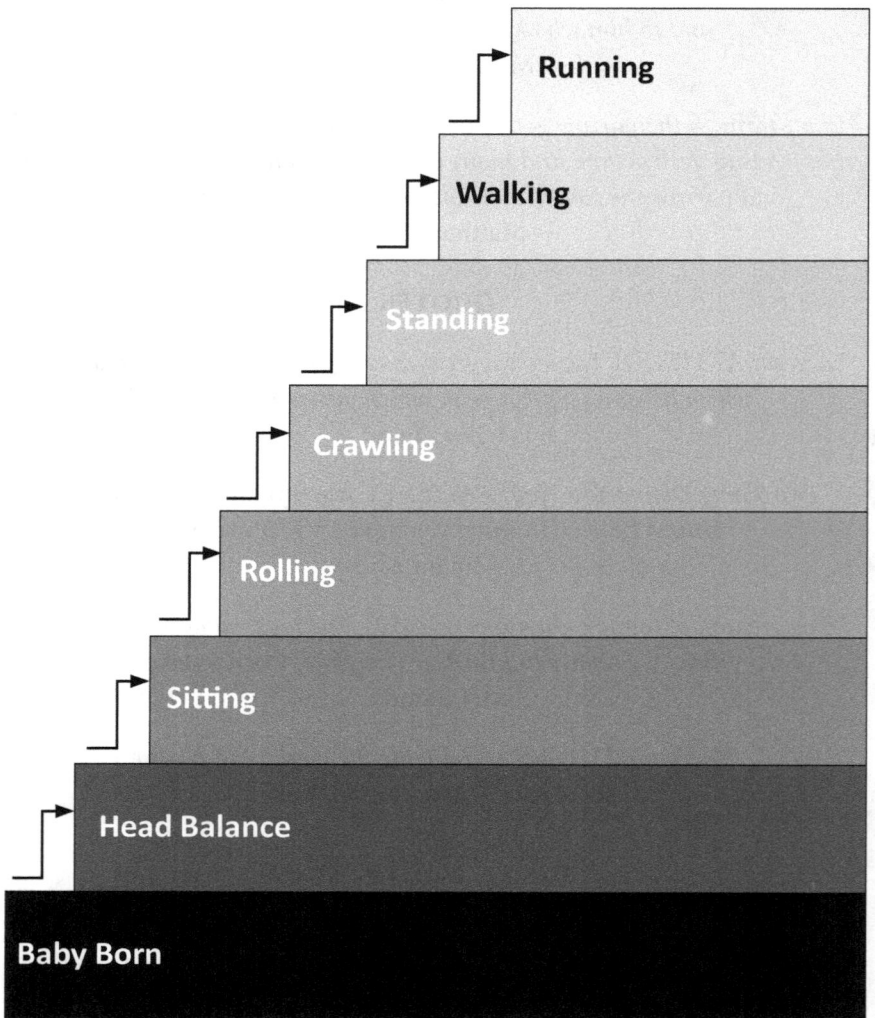

Running

Walking

Standing

Crawling

Rolling

Sitting

Head Balance

Baby Born

Get

BITTER

Or Get

BETTER

7. SUSTAIN Actions – Preserve

"Wealth gained by dishonesty will be diminished, but he who gathers by labor will increase."
– Proverbs 16:3

How do you keep motivation constantly? How do you sustain working for longer periods of time on your actions? How do you stick with it and prevent yourself from going low or running out? Again, you have to be consciously aware by having clarity and commitment to develop high levels of motivation.

SUSTAINING MOTIVATION = FOCUS (Attention) + ACTION (Effort)

ATTENTION

What are you focusing your mind on? What are you constantly thinking about? What are you paying attention to? The most effective way to force you to develop attention and concentration is by removing distractions. Remove the past, remove those negative thoughts, ideas or beliefs. When you are tranquil and calm, clarity will develop and eventually you will have organized thoughts. When you *have* clean and clear thoughts in your mind, they will be *followed* by having clean, clear and positive feeling and actions .

A focused mind and having clarity will give you much better, clearer goals, clearer planning and clearer priorities. Think on paper, set priorities and develop a to-do list – remember, single mind - single task. Higher attention will give you higher productivity to accomplish the results you want. Are you going to work longer? Work faster? Work on higher values? Work on your strengths? Group your tasks for quick accomplishment? Simplify your work?

Focus on Yourself and Your Relationships

How would you like to be remembered? What would you like to be seen as? Find three words that define who you really are so you can THINK at all times and keep it on your mind to change your ACTIONS. Do you want to be present? Do you want to be bold? Do you want to be energetic?

How would you like others to perceive you when connecting with your family and friends? Find three words that you can THINK and ACT ON to always remind you. Do you want to be loving? Do you want to be engaged? Do you want to be inspiring?

EFFORT

Are you really trying your best? Are you trying hard enough? Are you giving your best self? Are you putting in your best effort? The most effective way to force you to develop "effort" within is to continually challenge yourself. Challenge your mind through your thinking and thoughts, and challenge your body through your movement and actions.

CHALLENGE

Push yourself to new levels in all areas of your life. Stretch to higher steps and take it to a higher performance by engaging your mind and practicing daily. Be bolder and intentionally set meaningful challenges for yourself. Pick a goal so big and so audacious that it lifts you up constantly, every time you think about it. Be the change you want to see in your family and raise the bar, raise above mediocrity. Remember, small goals do not spark or sustain the imagination, drive or courage.

No PAIN. No GAIN.

<u>KEEPING</u> YOUR BEHAVIOR

You must focus and take action immediately to achieve your desired goals. Remember, you do not just have motivation, you can only GENERATE it from within. Once you start on "something", just concentrate on it for as long as you can while taking action at the same time. This will create momentum, and a movement will take place in your life.

If it doesn't

CHALLENGE

you

It doesn't

CHANGE

you

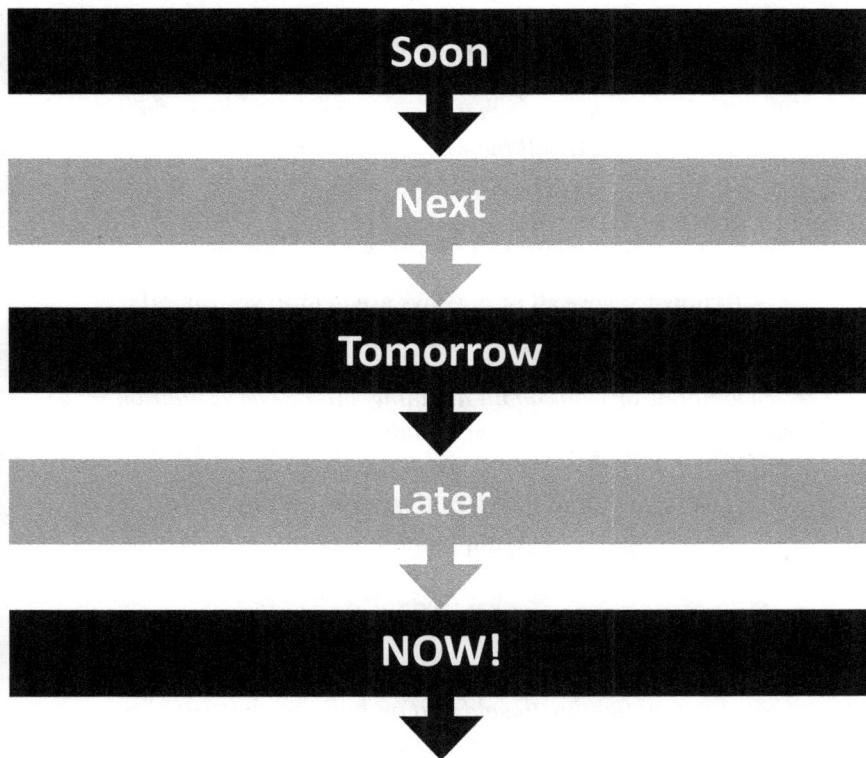

BIBLE

"The Apostle Paul said, '..but this one thing I do: forgetting what lies behind and reaching forward to what lies ahead.'"
– Philippians 3:13

<u>Don't look back; your future is greater than your past.</u>

"Yet, O Lord, you are our Father. We are the clay, you are the potter; we are all the work of your hand."
– ISAIAH 64:8 NIV

TAKE me, MOLD me, USE me, FILL me.

I know for sure all of my days are held in your hand, crafted into Your perfect plan.

"Do not be anxious about anything, but in every situation, through prayer and petition, with thanksgiving, present your requests to God. And the peace of God, which transcends all understanding, will guard your hearts and minds in Christ Jesus."
– Philippians 4:6-7

QUOTES

"The secret of CHANGE is to focus all of your energy, not on fighting the old, but on building the new."
– Socrates

"If you want to make the world a better place, take a look at yourself and make the CHANGE."
– Michael Jackson

"CHANGE is hard at first, MESSY in the middle and GORGEOUS at the end."
– Robin Sharma

"Growth is painful. CHANGE is painful. But nothing is as painful as staying stuck somewhere you don't belong."
– Mandy Hale

8. AMPLIFY Actions – Expand

*"How blessed is the man who finds wisdom, and the
man who gains understanding."*
– Proverbs 3:13

How do you grow your motivation to get actions done? How do you "multiply" your motivation to be more, to do more and to have more? How do your expand your motivation to reach the highest levels? You have to learn how to THINK to change your attitude and the RELATIONSHIPS within your environment.

AMPLIFY Motivation = THOUGHTS (Attitude) + RELATIONSHIPS (Environment)

THOUGHTS

You have to learn to control your thoughts at the conscious level as they will dictate how you will feel and, consequently, they will determine your actions. Your attitude is the combination of your thoughts, feeling and actions... and they all need to be positive.

RELATIONSHIPS

From an external and outside perspective, you have to have a relationship with other environments – with God and with the other people.

RELATIONSHIP WITH GOD

God created you. He is the creator. Connect with Him through prayer and He will answer your requests. He speaks through dreams, through ideas, through other people, through coincidences. Open yourself up and God will speak back to you through your own intuition.

MASTERMIND GROUPS

Do you want to amplify yourself? Magnify your mind? Gain higher levels of knowledge faster? What about doubling yourself, multiplying yourself, or even exponentially squaring yourself? Sharing information, knowledge, experiences and ideas with other people in mastermind group session is the answer.

"So encourage each other and build each other up."
– 1 Thessalonians 5:11a NLT

GROWING YOUR BEHAVIOR

You have one mind, and the capacity to understand and learn only one book at a time. A mastermind group is a team of people (let's say 10 people) who get together to share knowledge and learn from each other. Guess what? You will learn faster when you meet and interact with this select group of ten people. What could have taken you ten months to read ten books, you can learn in two hours. That is the power of mastermind groups. Now, even better and faster, is if you connect to God, to infinite intelligence, and you will be able to have the highest of all.

BIBLE

"There has never been the slightest doubt in my mind that the God who started this great work in you would keep at it and bring it to a flourishing finish on the very day Christ Jesus appears."
– Philippians 1:6 MSG

"Remain in Me, and I will remain in you. No branch can bear fruit by itself; it must remain on the vine. Neither can you bear fruit unless you remain in Me."
– John 15:4

"Much is required from those to whom much is given, and much more is required from those to whom much more is given."
– Luke 12:48b NLT

"Whatever you do, work at it with all your heart, as working for the Lord, not for men, since you know that you will receive an inheritance from the Lord as a reward. It is the Lord Christ you are serving."
– Colossians 3:23-24

"For it is God's will that by doing good you should silence the ignorant talk of foolish people."
– 1 Peter 2:15 NIV

QUOTES

"Two things that will define you. Your determination when you have nothing. Your ATTITUDE when you have everything."
– Unknown

"The harder you work, the harder it is to surrender."
– Vince Lombardi

"A strong, positive mental ATTITUDE will create more miracles than any wonder drug."
– Patricia Neal

"The only power we have in our life is our ATTITUDE and that makes all the difference."
– Mimi Ikonn

"Being HUMBLE is much more important than being WISE! Because God doesn't need a PROUD mouth that SPEAKS much. But a KIND heart that LISTENS."
– Unknown

"God knows exactly what you need, who you need, when you need it."
– Joel Osteen

REFLECTIONS

Your Attitude is vitally important and it will WIN over skill each and every time.

Stop searching. Start SERVING.

You don't have an attitude problem, you have a perception problem.

Turning
ME
To
WE

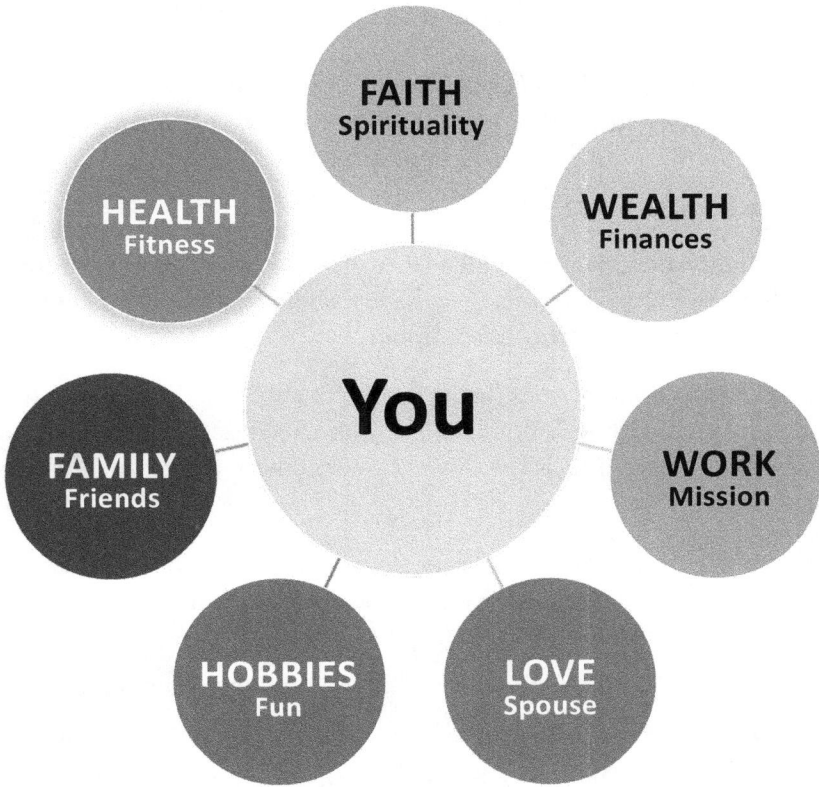

9. Seven Practices for Every Day

"Always be humble and gentle. Be patient with each other, making allowance for each other's faults because of your love."
– Ephesians 4:2

Become your best <u>self</u> to achieve your best <u>dreams</u>. Remember, you don't "have" motivation, you GENERATE it. The "mother" of motivation is CHOICE. Fire your will to set great habits. Sliding is faster than climbing, but everything truly worthwhile is uphill.

Start with intentional actions (being conscious about it), then those actions will be set and become "automatic" (in your subconscious mind) with no effort on your part. This is the way to have and keep a permanent change in any area of your life.

What areas of your life do you want to grow and improve? Why are they like that at this time? The answers to these questions usually come from three main sources:

- Lack of ATTENTION (your mind) and thinking about this area.
- Lack of AFFECTION (your heart) and connecting in this area.
- Lack of ACTIONS (your body) and activities or habits in this area.

These seven practices to master are based on a broad perspective to start changing you, for you to become your very best. Show the world the best version of yourself and once you become this person, you will be able to do more, to have more and to give more to others. The starting point is you.

1. BE HEALTHIER, WEALTHIER and HAPPIER

From the SOUL perspective – Prayer, Meditation, and Gratitude: Take time to pray to God, to be quiet and listen, to meditate and silence your mind for a few minutes. Feel and appreciate all things you have today. Be grateful to be alive. Appreciate what you have since you don't truly know what you've got until it's taken away from you... that's when it is too late.

From the MIND perspective – Reading, Writing and Thinking: Start reading positive books 30 minutes a day according to your desires and your profession. Write notes in a notebook and keep a journal to write down your ideas as well. Take time to think about you, about others, about your day.

From the HEART perspective – Listening to Music, Singing, Dancing: Start feeling the music, worshipping God, listening to your favorite songs and, if you can, sing and dance as it will stimulate your emotions.

From the BODY perspective – Nutrition, Exercise and Resting: Eating more greens and less carbohydrates is recommended. Exercising by doing cardio, strength, balance and flexibility movements. Resting by sleeping a full eight hours, taking 20 minutes naps, and taking a break every 50 minutes while doing any mental activity. Balance what you eat, drink and do.

2. GENERATE ENTHUSIASM

Start your day with happiness by generating enthusiasm from all four perspectives; the soul, mind, heart and body. Be grateful for a new day, about your life amongst others. Start reading positive books. Encourage yourself to listen to music and engage in the music with passion and emotion. Eat healthy food, take a walk outside and get eight hours of sleep.

3. FACE A FEAR OR DIFFICULTY

Challenge yourself by facing a difficulty every single day. Whenever it is hard, we usually want to do it last. Change your thinking and actions and be intentional and do those things first.

4. FOCUS ON THREE THINGS TO DO

Create just three things that you must do today. Productivity tasks that will make you grow and not just activities that make you busy. No matter what, start doing these things first thing in the morning, with no distractions.

5. ACT OF KINDNESS

Be intentional in asking yourself – how am I going to add value today? Focus on others, believe in people, believe in unconditional love, and make kindness be driven by your choice through your words and actions.

6. BE THE FIRST TO HELP

Be intentional by being the first to reach out a hand to help someone. People will always remember who was there to help and will never forget who was there to help them first. It doesn't need to be big, expensive or complicated, it just needs to be intentional.

7. SURPRISE PEOPLE WITH WORDS

Share with them how much they mean to you. Sometimes we live in a world that is too fast. We need to learn to stop for a moment and speak words of appreciation to others. You will make their day, their week, their month or even their life.

QUOTES

"One STEP in the right direction is worth 100 years of thinking about it."
– Harv Eker

"The only way to become happy is to make someone else happy."
– Mihail Veller

"We make a LIVING by what we GET, but we make a LIFE by what we GIVE."
– Winston Churchill

"If you do what you've always done, you'll get what you've always gotten."
– Tony Robbins

"No matter how many mistakes you make or how slow you progress, you're still way ahead of everyone who isn't trying."
– Tony Robbins

BIBLE

"And we know that in all things God works for the good of those who love him, who have been called according to his purpose."
– Romans 8:28

"So encourage each other and build each other up."
– 1 Thessalonians 5:11a NLT

"God has given each of us the ability to do certain things well."
– Romans 12:6a NLT

*"For we are God's masterpiece. He has created us anew in Christ Jesus,
so that we can do the good things he planned for us long ago."*
– Ephesians 2:10 NLT

REFLECTIONS

The most important asset you can build is YOURSELF.

DO your BEST and God will do the REST.

A better YOU will always create a better WORLD.

Maturity is not when we SPEAK big things but when we start to UNDERSTAND small things.

Until you change your THINKING, you will always recycle your EXPERIENCES.

Time is more valuable than Money. ENERGY is more valuable than time.

Whatever you do, or dream you can, BEGIN it. Boldness has genius and power and magic in it.

While we try to teach our children all about life, our children teach us what life is all about. Cuddling literally kills depression, relieves anxiety and strengthens the immune system.

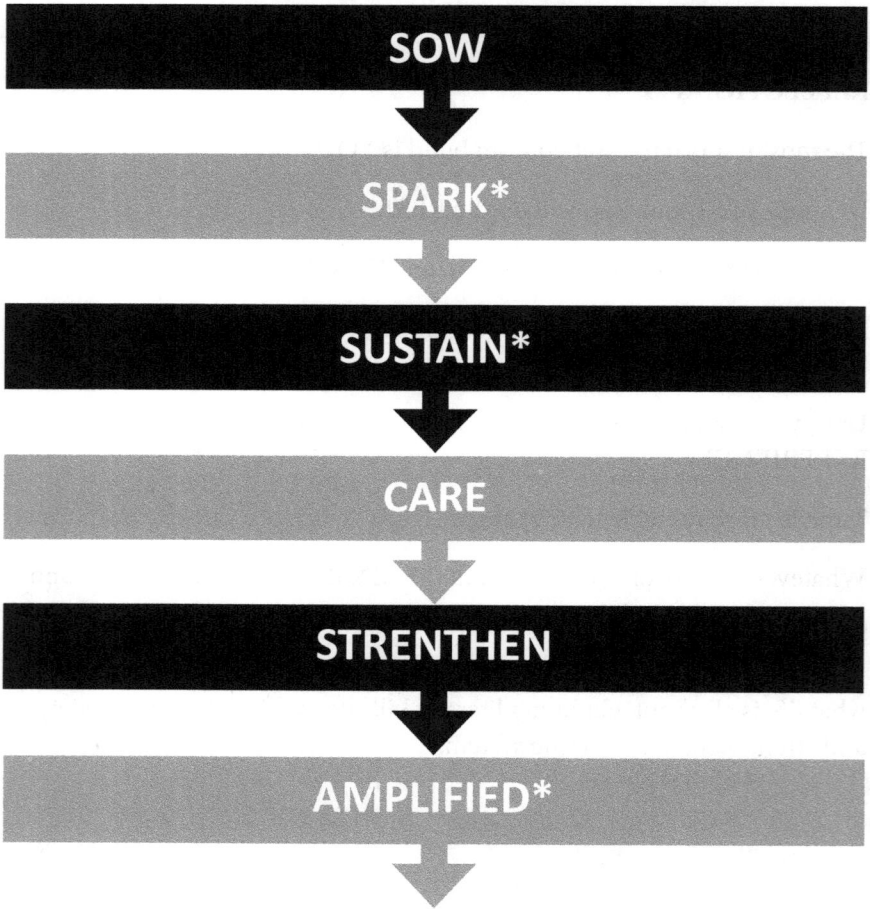

Are you making an
INCOME
making an
IMPACT

Conclusion

"Dear children, let us not love with words or speech
but with actions and in truth."
– 1 John 3:18

"Be still in the presence of the Lord, and <u>wait</u> patiently for him to act."
– Psalm 37:7 NLT

Presence Moves... Intellect! Awareness! Learning! Change!

"Do GOOD. And good will come to you."
– Unknown

"Love is patient and kind. Love is not jealous or boastful or proud
or rude. It does not demand its own way. It is not irritable, and it keeps
no record of being wronged. It does not rejoice about injustice
but rejoices whenever the truth wins out. Love never gives up, never loses
faith, is always hopeful, and endures through every circumstance."
– 1 CORINTHIANS 13: 4-7

What do you want in your life? It is a hard question to answer if you really think about it. Do you need ideas? Let's think outside the box... you have a problem, because big ideas come from everyday problems. Be observant as your eye Q is more important than your IQ, listen carefully as your ears are antennas for ideas, borrow an idea from a source and build it into a new idea, make connections by taking one thing and connecting it to another, make mistakes often as failures lead to great ideas, or just simply think and write your ideas down and let your imagination and inspiration flow.

In any moment of <u>decision</u> you only have two options. You either step forward to push yourself harder and grow or you stay and step backward for security. Choose to push, to never give up. Get a goal, a challenge to push yourself. Create a deadline to push you, to push yourself with self-discipline. Get others to push you, get competition to push you, get a tormentor to push you, and a mentor or coach to support you. Whatever you're doing in life just push yourself to the limit. Push yourself out of your comfort zones.

If you are on an island by yourself, burn your boat as people tend to succeed when they are faced with die or succeed decisions.

When you hit the wall, because you will, be persistent and persevere... climb over, dig under it, walk around it, take a hammer and hit it. Hit every minute, every hour, every day, every week, every month, every year... until you break through.

I believe in you. I believe you can do it. I believe you are unique.

You are **READY** now! Take action, improve and try new things. It's your time. You are ready for real growth in your life, for a new transition, for your next action. You are more than ready, so get started and just do it today. Don't be scared, don't worry, don't ask, don't stop, don't freeze, don't look for perfection. Just go for it and do it... and do it now, today, this present moment. Whatever it is; health, love, mission, hobbies, family, career, spirituality.

You are **CAPABLE**, you can do it! Believe in your ability to figure things out now. You already have the knowledge, skill, talent and ability to make it happen. You are a valuable human being. You have <u>VALUE</u> and you're very capable and competent to get it done.

You **DESERVE** good things; success, love, joy and abundance. You are worthy of great things in your life. Be out there and try new things, believe, and realize that you deserve it all. You deserve <u>CHANGE</u> and you are in this world for a purpose.

Be **OPEN** to trying, to learning, for getting feedback, for new opportunities. You don't have to know all the answers or all the solutions. Just by opening yourself to grow, to change and to learn you are ahead of most people who don't even try.

Be a **ROLE MODEL** for your children, for your children's children, for your family, for your generation, for your friends, for your neighbors, for your co-workers. Leave your footprints in this world. Create great memories and leave a legacy for them to remember.

Be **INTENTIONAL** with your thinking and your actions. Make a life of significance. Be DIFFERENT and make a DIFFERENCE in this world. Do significant things. Become the author of your own story. Leave a footprint in your book of life. You BE you. You may have a difficult conversation to make, but start now, take action, take control and do it quickly, calmly, privately and thoughtfully.

Be **PERSISTENT**, keep pushing, keep trying, keep moving. Your struggles through difficulty, uncertainty, chaos and rejection are bringing you closer and closer to your dreams and goals. Be persistent and never ever give up. Every time you take a step, think a positive thought, experience a wonderful feeling, make a good choice or practice a small discipline, you are moving one step closer.

Do MAKE MISTAKES, make amazing mistakes, make mistakes nobody's ever made before. When you make mistakes, you are trying new things, making new things, changing yourself, pushing yourself, learning, growing, living and changing the people around you, changing the world and changing humankind.

The secret to a GOOD LIFE is to never stop SMILING, DREAMING, LOVING, HUGGING, HOLDING, SEARCHING, THANKING, FEELING, LEARNING, PLAYING, LAUGHING, THINKING, WISHING, FORGIVING, HEALING, EXPRESSING, APPRECIATING, BELIEVING, CHERISHING, CREATING, HOPING, LIVING.

My goal was not to see how many books I could sell, how much money I could make or even how many people I could reach; my sole intention was for you to take action. Not to say "what a lovely book" but to say, "I WILL DO SOMETHING ABOUT MY LIFE." It's better to help people to START a journey than to give a solution. How many success stories do you need to hear before you write your own story?

Find God and you are in heaven on earth; do not find God and you are in hell. The more money, power and happiness you have, the greater the chance that you fall... and you will, and you will get hurt. However, it is the pain from that fall that will make you go to God.

I see God responding to those who genuinely call out in Him in prayer. That's why the Bible tells us to *"pray without ceasing"* (1 Thessalonians 5:17) because "*earnest prayer of a righteous person has great power and produces wonderful results*" (James 5:16). I pray that God will use you to make a positive impact on the world around you.

Help people, whether you're being paid or not. Don't hold back. Give back. Be different, make a difference and continue to have a life of significance. Today, make time for others that you will be grateful for tomorrow.

Live a life to remember. Be intentional and record the moment. If you are a son or daughter, go and interview your dad and mom. Ask them deep questions about life, about love and about what really matters. "Dad, how would you like to be remembered? What would you like me to think and do when you are no longer with me?" If you are a father or mother, write a letter to God for your son and daughter and then read it aloud directly to them. "Dear God, Thank you for the lovely father I have, for always being there for me, for teaching me about love." Do it now. This will change your life and the life of your loved ones.

Today will never come back. You will never get this day back, ever. Make your moments count and create the life that you really want. Create a legacy that you want to be remembered and to be known. Live, Love and make a difference today how you want to be remembered tomorrow.

I strive to be in a position to give. I want to have so much that I am not a borrower or a lender, I'm a giver expecting nothing in return. Today, I am giving you the very best I have to give.

I would not recommend a program but I would recommend people.

As a closing, to you, the reader: thank you, thank you and thank you for reading this book, for investing your time, energy and money in you, for trying to improve your life, for looking for ways to help others. Please never, ever give up on your dreams. It may not happen when you want it to, but one day your dream will come true if you keep pushing yourself. I really hope that I helped you, that I contributed some, that I did my part to pour some knowledge into your head and put a seed in your heart; a seed that will grow day after day and one day the fruit will be there. Again, my immense gratitude to you. Be loving. Be positive. Be kind and, above all, be humble.

Make the REST of your life, the BEST of your life. Do your best and let God do the rest.

Let's work together. I am here to help you. I want to add value to you. I want you to discover your potential. Together we can win.

My purpose in life is growing and to help you grow so you can reach your potential as well. My hope is that you will find more meaning in this wonderful life. May God bless you.

Juan Carlos Arzola
Weston, Florida
June 2016

About the Author

Juan Carlos Arzola, an international coach, trainer, consultant, author and speaker, has been mentored by some of the best in the industry of Personal Growth and Achievement. He has been coached, trained and mentored by John C. Maxwell, Bob Proctor, Brian Tracy, Tony Robbins, Brendon Burchard, Wayne Dyer, Deepak Chopra, Dave Ramsey among others. Juan Carlos Arzola works with his clients to learn and move from past limitations, to live and embrace what is possible in the present and to prepare for a better future, not only of success but of significance as well.

A big believer in becoming the best that you can be. His enthusiasm is believable and contagious. You will be entertained and encouraged at the same time. Readers, clients and audiences across the world have left with their hearts pumping and their minds full of great and concrete ideas that can be easily applied immediately to their daily lives.

A portion of the royalties earned from *The Success Start* will be donated to Mission For The Nations Foundation (www.missionsforthenations.org), a not for profit Christian organization in Dominican Republic dedicated to providing education, health and food to children.

APPENDIX

4 x 4 CLARITY FORMULA

✔ BE **more** of certain way: *loving, caring*

✔ BE **less** of a certain way: *complain, judging*

✔ **START** BEING the way that you are not being: *being helpful, kind*

✔ **STOP** BEING the way that you are being: *being rude, arrogant*

✔ DO **more** of a certain things (increase activities) greater value, rewards, satisfaction

✔ DO **less** of a certain things (reduce activities) decide to discontinue, hurtful

✔ **START** DOING things that you are not doing (good & new activities) new choices, learn new skills

✔ **STOP** DOING things that you are doing (bad & old activities) old habits, evaluate life

✔ HAVE **more** of certain things: *love, money*

✔ HAVE **less** of certain things: *bad relationships, debts*

✔ **START** HAVING things that you do not have: *passion, happiness*

✔ **STOP** HAVING things that you have: *sadness, confusion*

✔ GIVE **more** of certain things: *love, money*

✔ GIVE **less** of certain things: *bad relationships, debts*

✔ **START** GIVING things that you do not have: *passion, happiness*

✔ **STOP** GIVING things that you have: *sadness, confusion*

Instructions:

1. Think and Reflect

2. Write all 16 steps

3. Print it & Post it

4. Read it aloud daily

5. Visualize it twice a day

6. Evaluate, Update & Adjust

7. Write only the first thing on each area of your TO BE, TO DO, TO HAVE, TO GIVE (1. line marked by this symbol ◄)

8. Print it and hang it on your computer, mirror, kitchen, bathroom, office or wherever you'll SEE it daily.

9. READ it aloud every morning as you wake up + every night before you go to bed for 3 weeks. Mark each day as you progress.

10. WRITE this statements again on a separate paper daily and SHARE it with family and friends as well.

CLARITY LIFE PLANNER

<table>
<tr><td>

3 things you want to **BE more** of a certain way:

1. _____ ◄
2. _____
3. _____

3 things you want to **START** BEING, that you're not:

1. _____ ◄
2. _____
3. _____

</td><td>

3 things you want to **BE less** of a certain way:

1. _____ ◄
2. _____
3. _____

3 things you want to **STOP** BEING, that you are now

1. _____ ◄
2. _____
3. _____

</td></tr>
</table>

<table>
<tr><td>

3 things you want to **DO more** of certain things:

1. _____ ◄
2. _____
3. _____

3 things you want to **START** DOING, that you're not:

1. _____ ◄
2. _____
3. _____

</td><td>

3 things you want to **DO less** of certain things:

1. _____ ◄
2. _____
3. _____

3 things you want to **STOP** DOING, that you do now:

1. _____ ◄
2. _____
3. _____

</td></tr>
</table>

3 things you want to **HAVE more** of:	3 things you want to **HAVE less** of:
1. _____ ◄	1. _____ ◄
2. _____	2. _____
3. _____	3. _____
3 things you want to **START** HAVING, that you don't:	3 things you want to **STOP** HAVING, that you have now:
1. _____ ◄	1. _____ ◄
2. _____	2. _____
3. _____	3. _____

3 things you want to **GIVE more** of certain things:	3 things you want to **GIVE less** of certain things:
1. _____ ◄	1. _____ ◄
2. _____	2. _____
3. _____	3. _____
3 things you want to **START** GIVING, that you don't give	3 things you want to **STOP** GIVING, that you give now:
1. _____ ◄	1. _____ ◄
2. _____	2. _____
3. _____	3. _____

MY SUCCESS LIFE PLAN

1. BE	1st Week	2nd Week	3rd Week
I want to BE more _____	✓✓✓✓✓✓	✓✓✓✓✓✓	✓✓✓✓✓✓
I want to BE less _____	✓✓✓✓✓✓	✓✓✓✓✓✓	✓✓✓✓✓✓
I want to START being _____	✓✓✓✓✓✓	✓✓✓✓✓✓	✓✓✓✓✓✓
I want to STOP being _____	✓✓✓✓✓✓	✓✓✓✓✓✓	✓✓✓✓✓✓

1. DO	1st Week	2nd Week	3rd Week
I want to DO more _____	✓✓✓✓✓✓	✓✓✓✓✓✓	✓✓✓✓✓✓
I want to DO less _____	✓✓✓✓✓✓	✓✓✓✓✓✓	✓✓✓✓✓✓
I want to START doing _____	✓✓✓✓✓✓	✓✓✓✓✓✓	✓✓✓✓✓✓
I want to STOP doing _____	✓✓✓✓✓✓	✓✓✓✓✓✓	✓✓✓✓✓✓

1. HAVE	1st Week	2nd Week	3rd Week
I want to HAVE more _____	✓✓✓✓✓✓	✓✓✓✓✓✓	✓✓✓✓✓✓
I want to HAVE less _____	✓✓✓✓✓✓	✓✓✓✓✓✓	✓✓✓✓✓✓
I want to START having _____	✓✓✓✓✓✓	✓✓✓✓✓✓	✓✓✓✓✓✓
I want to STOP having _____	✓✓✓✓✓✓	✓✓✓✓✓✓	✓✓✓✓✓✓

1. GIVE	1st Week	2nd Week	3rd Week
I want to GIVE more _____	✓✓✓✓✓✓	✓✓✓✓✓✓	✓✓✓✓✓✓
I want to GIVE less _____	✓✓✓✓✓✓	✓✓✓✓✓✓	✓✓✓✓✓✓
I want to START giving _____	✓✓✓✓✓✓	✓✓✓✓✓✓	✓✓✓✓✓✓
I want to STOP giving _____	✓✓✓✓✓✓	✓✓✓✓✓✓	✓✓✓✓✓✓

GRATITUDE

List 10 things you are grateful RIGHT NOW.

1. _____

2. _____

3. _____

4. _____

5. _____

6. _____

7. _____

8. _____

9. _____

10. _____

GOALS

Write a letter to yourself 5 years from RIGHT NOW.

I am so happy and grateful today that...

I am _____

_____

_____

_____

_____

I do _____

_____

_____

_____

_____

I have _____

_____

_____

I give _____

_____

_____

_____

CLARITY Actions

What are 5 things that you LEARNED and DECIDED by reading this book?

1. _____

_____

_____

2. _____

_____

_____

3. _____

_____

_____

4. _____

_____

_____

5. _____

_____

_____

CLARITY Ways

What actions are you going to START doing?_____

_____

_____

_____

_____

What actions are you going to STOP doing?_____

_____

_____

_____

_____

What actions are you going to do MORE? _____

_____

_____

_____

_____

What actions are you going to do LESS? _____

_____

_____

_____

_____

CLARITY Lists

What is your TO DO list? _____

_____

_____

_____

_____

What is your NOT TO DO list? _____

_____

_____

_____

_____

What is your NOT NOW TO DO list? _____

_____

_____

_____

_____

What is your SUCCESS list? _____

_____

_____

_____

_____

CLARITY Journals

<u>REFLECTIVE</u> Journal: Focus on PAST, be a LEARNER!

What did I learn? _____

_____

_____

_____

_____

_____

<u>IDEAS</u> Journal: Focus on PRESENT, be CREATIVE!

What's in your mind now? _____

_____

_____

_____

_____

_____

<u>DREAM</u> Journal: Focus on FUTURE, be a DREAMER!

What are your goals and objectives? _____

_____

_____

_____

_____

_____

RECOMMENDED READING

Think and Grow Rich	Napoleon Rich
As a Man Thinketh	James Allen
Man's Search For Meaning	Victor Franckl
The Science of Getting Rich	Wallace Wattles
You2	Price Pritchett
Your Invisible Power	Genervieve Behrend
The Power of Now	Eckhart Tolle
The Magic of Thinking Big	David Schwartz
How To Win Friends & Influence People	Dale Carnegie
The Richest Man in Babylon	George S. Clason
The Law of Success in Sixteen Lessons	Napoleon Hill
The Greatest Salesman in the World	Og mandino
Thinking into Results	Bob Proctor
The Art of Acting	Stella Adler
The Impersonal Life	Joseph Benner
The Purpose Driven Life	Rick Warren
Psycho-Cybernetics	Maxwell Maltz, M.D.
The Mastery of Love	Don Miguel Ruiz
A Better Way to Live	Og mandino
Inner Wisdom	Louise L. Hay
The Power of Intention: Learning to Co-create Your World	Dr. Wayne W. Dyer

WHAT'S NEXT

You've implemented all of the tactics in this guide and have likely witnessed some impressive results. Now what?

Learning, growing, changing and transforming isn't a once-and-done effort. You need to continue to spark, sustain and amplify your motivation and inspiration in all areas of your life.

There are dozens of great resources out there to put you on the path to a successful life, such as our website **www.JuanCarlosArzola.com**. Putting the time in to expand your knowledge will yield awesome results.

And remember, my team is just a <u>phone call, email or social media</u> away!

Connect Online at JUANCARLOS.LIVE

JUAN CARLOS ARZOLA

BE KIND. DO GOOD. HAVE LESS. GIVE MORE

HOW HAS THIS BOOK HELPED YOU?
We want to hear from you!

Send us an email at info@juancarlosarzola.com

Want more tips and strategies to create the life of your dreams?

Connect with us on our social media channels.

https://www.facebook.com/JuanCarlosArzolacom

https://twitter.com/juancarlosarzol

https://www.youtube.com/c/JuanCarlosArzola

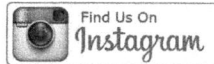

https://www.instagram.com/juancarlos.live/

https://www.pinterest.com/JuanCarlosLive/

https://www.linkedin.com/in/juancarlosarzola

NOTES

NOTES

NOTES

NOTES

NOTES

NOTES

NOTES

NOTES

NOTES